A
PICTORIAL
HISTORY
OF THE
MOVIE
MUSICAL

A
Pictorial
History
of the
Movie
Musical

by JOHN SPRINGER

introduction by GENE KELLY

CASTLE BOOKS

This edition is published by
Castle Books, a division of
Book Sales Inc. of Secaucus, N.J.

Manufactured in the United States of America

ISBN 0-89009-526-4

This Book Is Dedicated To —

- The second chorus cutie from the right who just happens to know all the steps when the star twists her ankle at the last minute before curtain . . .

- The drab little secretary who takes off her glasses — and, presto, she's a pin-up girl . . .

- The heiress (or princess or world-famed type) who is mistaken for her own maid by that nice young man . . .

- The poor girl who is mistaken for the heiress (or princess or world-famed type) by that nice young man . . .

- The girl-shy student who tutors the college football hero to a passing mark in chemistry . . .

- The kids who put on a variety show to raise money for the sweet old lady who is going to be evicted (or the little girl who will go into an orphanage . . . or the old professor whose dream is a new school library, etc.) . . .

- The old music master (or father of the musician) who conducts weakly from his hospital bed as the radio brings his protégé's concert debut . . .

- The lovesick sailor (soldier, airman) who sings about his sweetheart on the empty deck (barracks, hangar) which instantly becomes crowded with dancing girls — all looking like his sweetheart . . .

- The cowboy who sings to his horse on the lonely prairie — all alone except for the 200-piece orchestra which is suddenly heard in accompaniment . . .

- The small-time vaudeville team who split up when one is wanted by Ziegfeld but get back together after the rising one gets the big head and flops . . .

- The personality-plus girl who always says, "Listen, kids — I have an idea!" . . .

Without their help — and the help of all like them — these movies could not have been made, and this book could not have been written.

Acknowledgments

Thanks for assistance in securing some of the pictures in this book to:

Joseph Abeles (Friedman-Abeles); Alan Bader (Twentieth Century-Fox); Mike Berman (Paramount); Philip Gerard (Universal); Richard Griffith (Museum of Modern Art); Terry Hamill (United Artists); Jack Hamilton (*Look*); Hy Hollinger (Paramount); Norman Kaphan (M-G-M); Charles Levy (Walt Disney); John Newfield (Columbia); Mark Nichols; Ernest Parmentier (*Screen Facts*); Ruth Pologe (American International); Leo Wilder (Warner Brothers); and Dick Winters (M-G-M).

Special gratitude to Martin Burden for a particular suggestion for the writing of this book; and unlimited appreciation to Gene Kelly for his introduction.

Song listings following Chapters One through Four and in the Appendix were checked with *The Blue Book of Hollywood Musicals* by Jack Burton, published in 1953 by Century House, and also with *Screen Facts* compiled and edited by Ernest Parmentier, and *Popular Music* edited by Nat Shapiro, published 1964 by Adrian Press.

Contents

Introduction

by GENE KELLY

I've been a devotee of the movie musical for a long time — long, long before I had any idea that I would ever be associated with that world myself. From Busby Berkeley's wildest flights of fancy to a Chevalier song done straight, before a backdrop, from Shirley Temple's childish piping to Jeanette MacDonald hitting a high "C," from Ruby Keeler and Ginger Rogers to Eleanor Powell. And don't forget Bing Crosby and Alice Faye, Al Jolson and Dick Powell, and Grace Moore — how the names come back. And Judy Garland — wonderful Judy. And, of course, Astaire! Always Astaire!

But there is more to the movie musical than just a series of particularly happy memories. It's one of the few peculiarly American art forms and, at its best, it certainly is art. The French can make crime films that equal or surpass ours, comedy is polished by the British, and even the American Western has been taken over with some success by the Germans. But, outside of a few pleasant Jessie Matthews British films of the thirties, what movie musical even worth noting has been produced under any auspices except Hollywood's?

If there has been a publication that has given more than a passing nod to the world of musical movies, it has escaped me. That's why it is a special joy to find such a comprehensive and entertaining treatment here. Historically, this book puts things in their proper perspective, and the author understands the implications and growth of the musical cinema with attention to the effects and interplay that some innovations have had on those which were to follow.

The subject is treated with understanding and with affection. And, knowing the author, I'm not surprised. John Springer knows as much about movies as anyone I've met, and his love for the movie world is evident. It's a delight to listen in on a session in which John and another aficionado — say, the brilliant Adolph Green — reminisce about the movies they've known and loved and attempt, with small success, to stump each other on obscure bits of information about them.

This book, to me, is like one of those sessions. It is knowledgeable and authoritative and it traces its history with perception. But, above all, it's fun — fun in the nostalgia it evokes, in the rushing recollections it so vividly conjures up, but also, I should think, enjoyable even to those whose own memories of musical movies extend little farther back than *Mary Poppins* and the Beatles.

Every so often, they tell us that musical movies are dead. And always there comes a *Forty-Second Street* or a Crosby or Astaire, a *West Side Story*, a Julie Andrews to prove them dead wrong. This book reflects that — it doesn't merely look backward with fondness and warmth, it looks ahead with excitement and optimism.

I'm glad to be a part of the world it celebrates.

A
PICTORIAL
HISTORY
OF THE
MOVIE
MUSICAL

CHAPTER ONE

100% All Talking!
All Singing! All Dancing!

John Gilbert and Mae Murray whirled through the *Merry Widow Waltz* and the neighborhood movie-house piano tinkled its accompaniment — just as it had for Valentino's tango and Clara Bow's first jazz-baby Charleston.

LONG BEFORE Al Jolson and the Brothers Warner broke the sound barrier, music was important to the movies. Was there ever even the tiniest Bijou Dream on the most ramshackle back street which did not have its own piano player beating out an accompaniment to the silent antics of the Keystone Kops, the cowboy heroes, and the damsels in distress? The pianists controlled the music for the movies in those days, and "Hearts and Flowers" could be the accompaniment for Fatty Arbuckle's funniest adventures, if the piano player felt like playing "Hearts and Flowers."

Some of the bigger pictures sent out "suggested musical scores" to be played with their films. "The Perfect Song," more famous years later as the "Amos 'n' Andy" radio theme song, was originally suggested music for *Birth of a Nation.*

But it was later — in the days when records and radio could help in promotion — that "theme songs" written especially for certain movies became popular. So we had "Ramona" and "Charmaine," "Jeannine, I Dream of Lilac Time," and eventually ditties as far-fetched as "Woman Disputed, I Love You."

The first sound picture changed all that. Al Jolson got down on one knee and sang to his "Mammy" and the singing came right from the screen. What a miracle! The musical movie was born.

Then came the era of the backstage musicals — "All Talking * All Singing * All Dancing!" according to the billboards — and before long you had to sing a torch song or tap a waltz clog in order to get ahead in Hollywood. Some well-established silent stars managed to conquer the new medium. More came from their own worlds of Broadway, vaudeville, night clubs, and radio.

Some of the best-known didn't make a dent in talkies. Others caught on immediately. But musical movies kept going strong — at least, for a while. To add to backstage movies, there were night club movies and college movies, all-star revues, operettas, and adaptations of Broadway musical comedies. But they glutted the market. By mid-1930, people were staying away from them and exhibitors were putting up signs to announce "This is not a musical."

And it was all over — or close to that — for two years, or until *Forty-Second Street* started the whole cycle over again.

But those first years of talking movies are notable ones for the musical movie buff. It's about them that this section deals — about the pictures and the stars who sang and danced: Al Jolson and Bessie Love, Charles Farrell and Janet Gaynor, Nancy Carroll and Buddy Rogers, Chevalier and Jeanette MacDonald and the early Dietrich and all the rest. It was the "100% All Talking * All Singing * All Dancing!" period — fun while it lasted, even more fun to be remembered.

Dolores Del Rio as "Evangeline"

Nancy Carroll in *Abie's Irish Rose*

Came the Mighty Wurlitzer, and even full orchestras, for the grander cinema cathedrals. And came the theme song. Movies still didn't talk, but when you saw Charles Farrell make love to Janet Gaynor, you heard her song, "Diane." Or Colleen Moore dreamed of Gary Cooper while the organ played "Jeannine, I Dream of Lilac Time," Nancy Carroll was "Rosemary," Vilma Banky "Marie," and Dolores Del Rio had theme songs for several of her ladies—"Charmaine," "Ramona," and "Evangeline."

Janet Gaynor and Charles Farrell in *Seventh Heaven*

Colleen Moore and Gary Cooper in *Lilac Time*

Vilma Banky in *The Awakening*

15

Richard Dix in *Redskin*

Norma Talmadge and Gilbert Roland in *Woman Disputed*

The theme songs finally became ridiculous, when Norma Talmadge and Gilbert Roland emoted in *Woman Disputed* to the strains of "Woman Disputed, I Love You" and when the song from Richard Dix's *Redskin* asked, "Redskin, Why Are You Blue?" But suddenly theme songs were out. For along came Jolson — and movies not only talked, but sang.

16

Al Jolson's *The Jazz Singer* was a terrible picture even then — trite, corny, and with a characterization of pure hambone by the great Al. But that October night in 1927 when it was first shown was a night that made movie history. Because Al talked a little and sang a lot ("Mammy," "Toot-Toot-Tootsie," "Kol Nidre"). And, before you could say "Vitaphone," all the movies were talking — and singing, too.

Jolson and May McAvoy in *The Jazz Singer*

Jolson was always a great entertainer. But he was something less than a great screen star. After *The Jazz Singer*, he made a few forgettable quickies. But his only other big movie hit was *The Singing Fool,* in which he sobbed out the syrupy "Sonny Boy" to Davey Lee.

17

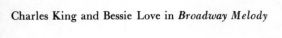
Charles King and Bessie Love in *Broadway Melody*

The first real movie musical — "100% All Talking * All Singing * All Dancing!" they advertised it, and those which followed — was *The Broadway Melody* in 1929. It had its own score by Nacio Herb Brown and Arthur Freed, and it was a good one (the title song, "You Were Meant For Me," "Wedding of the Painted Doll"). The story, about sister chorus girls and their singer boy friend, set the style for backstage movie musicals. And the picture briefly revived the fading careers of silent sweeties Bessie Love and Anita Page and gave a vaudevillian, Charles King, his brief moment in the movie limelight.

Anita Page, Charles King, and Bessie Love in *Broadway Melody*

Charles King, Bessie Love, Mary Doran, Anita Page, and Jed Prouty in *Broadway Melody*

In the wake of *The Broadway Melody* came other backstage musicals. Now even a tight little stage melodrama like *Broadway* had its big spectacular sequence when it came to the screen. Glenn Tryon played the hoofer in the movie version.

Glenn Tryon in *Broadway*

Nick Lukas and Ann Pennington in *Gold Diggers of Broadway*

A new ingredient was color — a garish, post-card color that hurt your eyes but made the musical numbers even more splashy. It "dressed up" such numbers as the "Painting the Clouds With Sunshine" spot from *Gold Diggers of Broadway* (sung by Nick Lukas, danced by Ann Pennington). Nancy Welford, Winnie Lightner, Lilyan Tashman, and Conway Tearle carried the story line, such as it was.

Lukas, Pennington, Albert Gran, Winnie Lightner, Nancy Welford, Conway Tearle, and Lilyan Tashman in *Gold Diggers of Broadway*

It was only a step from "all talking, all singing, all dancing, all color" and slim story line to "all star" and no story at all. The "revue era" was short, really just long enough for each of the big studios to come out with its own show. They were fun in their silly way — the artistic level being approximately that of a high-school presentation but maybe not quite so professional. Most elaborate was M-G-M's *Hollywood Revue*, which included such "treasures" as Marie Dressler in an underwater "ballet," Norma Shearer and John Gilbert doing the balcony scene from *Romeo and Juliet*, and a whole flock of stars (Buster Keaton, Marion Davies, Joan Crawford, and George K. Arthur, among others) in the "Singin' in the Rain" finale.

The Brox Sisters, Buster Keaton, Marion Davies, Joan Crawford, and George K. Arthur in *Hollywood Revue*

If M-G-M had "Singin' in the Rain," Warner Brothers would go them one better in its *Show of Shows*. So we were given "Singin' in the Bathtub" with the madly mugging Winnie Lightner as the "singing star." And if M-G-M could have "Romeo," Warners would shove in Shakespeare, too — John Barrymore in a soliloquy from *Richard II*.

Since Universal didn't have very many big names of its own, it imported Paul Whiteman and his band to headline *The King of Jazz*. John Murray Anderson made it all look fairly spectacular. Buried in the cast were a sing- ing threesome, The Rhythm Boys. If the Rhythm Boy at left looks familiar, he should. A gentleman by the name of Crosby — Bing, that is.

Paramount on Parade gave you everything from a singing Ruth Chatterton to Nancy Carroll (above) dancing out of a shoe. Also present: a group of gay blades (Richard Arlen, James Hall, Phillips Holmes, David Newell, Gary Cooper) and their ladies (Fay Wray, Jean Arthur, Joan Peers, Virginia Bruce, Mary Brian) and a frantic classroom with pupils Mitzi Green and Jackie Searle being taught to boop-boop-a-doop by teacher Helen Kane.

HEAR RAMON NOVARRO SING
COUNTRY OF ORIGIN U.S.A.

Talkies presented little hazard to some silent stars. Everyone knew that Ramon Novarro's physique was ideal for stripping as "The Pagan," but it was a pleasant surprise to find his singing voice adequate for the sultry strains of "Pagan Love Song." Dorothy Janis was his leading lady.

Sue Carol about to start the "Breakaway" in *Fox Movietone Follies.* Miss Carol wasn't much of a singer but, from sheet-music covers, you'd think her one of the era's top musical-comedy ladies. She "inspired" such songs as "Sweet Sue," "Kiss Waltz," and "Three Little Words."

Bebe Daniels and John Boles could sing, too, and, to prove it, they did a screen version of the popular Ziegfeld show, *Rio Rita*.

Gloria Swanson stuck to drama in pictures like *The Trespasser* (with Robert Ames, Kay Hammond, Wally Albright) but, just to show that she could, she included songs like "Love, Your Magic Spell Is Everywhere" and "Come to Me."

Pola Negri sang, too, in *A Woman Commands* with Roland Young. Although the song was the sensuous "Paradise," it came too late for Pola's diving popularity.

Clara Bow was typical of the silent screen star who tried, but just couldn't make it, in musicals. That sailor at the far right is Rex Bell, whom she married, and, yes, the boy right next to her is Fredric March.

One who adjusted well to the movie musicals was the dainty Janet Gaynor. With her long-time screen romance, Charles Farrell, she started out with *Sunny Side Up* with its memorable DeSylva, Brown, and Henderson score. There were other Gaynor-Farrell musicals but, by the time George Gershwin wrote a score for them, the musical vogue was waning. And neither the picture, *Delicious*, nor the Gershwin score was very good.

Gaynor, Charles Farrell, and Leila Hyams in *Delicious*

The All-American boy of the movie musical was Buddy Rogers. Buddy managed to be a male ingénue, even surrounded by ladies in lingerie like Josephine Dunn, Carol (not yet with a final 'e') Lombard, Kathryn Crawford, and Virginia Bruce. That picture was *Safety in Numbers,* best remembered for its still popular George Marion-Richard Whiting song "My Future Just Passed."

Buddy also romanced in song with a perky brunette named Lillian Roth, long before her *I'll Cry Tomorrow* miseries.

29

But by far the most memorable mate for Buddy's musical adventures was the delectable Nancy Carroll. They were a highly popular team in such musicals as *Close Harmony*, *Illusion*, and *Follow Through*, with Zelma O'Neal and Jack Haley as the secondary duo in the latter.

30

Hal Skelly and Carroll in *Dance of Life*

Nancy Carroll on the *Shopworn Angel* set

The red-haired, round-faced, blue-eyed Nancy Carroll hit the screen at just about the time silents were turning into talkies. She was, in fact, the first real star developed by talkies. Even most of her earliest silent pictures — *Abie's Irish Rose,* for instance — had

Stanley Smith, Carroll, and Mitzi Green in *Honey*

32

Smith, Carroll, and Wallace MacDonald in *Sweetie*

Nancy Carroll in *Shopworn Angel*

sound and songs. And she came along just in time to be the first real movie "dream girl" of this writer. Critic Walter Kerr once confessed that his most poignant memory of the early talkies was of Nancy Carroll dancing

and singing a jazzy little song, "Precious Little Thing Called Love," while tears stain her face as she visualizes Gary Cooper being killed in war. That was in *Shopworn Angel* — and it's a personal high spot, too.

Gary Cooper and Nancy Carroll in *Shopworn Angel*

Nancy Carroll sang in a funny, cooing, but wholly charming little voice. Her dancing was pleasant at best. But she was pretty and cute and, when the occasion called for it (as in *Dance of Life* and *Shopworn Angel*), an exceptionally good dramatic actress. There were *Sweetie* and *Honey* and others, with and without Buddy Rogers. And the songs — "Sweeter Than Sweet" and "Peach of a Pair,"

"True Blue Lou," "I Want to Go Places and Do Things," "Button Up Your Overcoat," "Sing You Sinners." Some of these she didn't even sing. But they were all in Nancy Carroll movies.

She switched to drama and became a top actress (*Devil's Holiday, Laughter,* etc.) before the vogue for musicals wore off.

Rudy Vallee had his radio, record, and vaudeville audiences swooning, but they just laughed when he tried to act in *Vagabond Lover*. Sally Blane appeared opposite him.

From radio, nightclubs, the theatre, and vaudeville came the big names to cash in on this new boom. In most cases, they did their picture and took the next train back to New York. Texas Guinan, for instance, may have been "The Queen of the Nightclubs," but her movie was a dud. And although she urged "a big hand" for him, nobody paid much attention to the slick-haired young hoofer either. Not until a couple of years later, that is. Then George Raft flipped a quarter and became a star.

Beatrice Lillie may be the funniest woman in the world, but she just can't seem to break the celluloid barrier. *Are You There?*, her first talkie, was a disaster.

Harry Richman fared only slightly better than Vallee — even with Joan Bennett as his leading lady and an Irving Berlin score — in *Puttin' on the Ritz*.

Harry Richman, Ted Sloman, James Gleason, and Joan Bennett on the set of *Puttin' on the Ritz*

Lillie's old stage buddy, Gertrude Lawrence, made out no better in her talkie debut, *Battle of Paris*.

Gertrude Lawrence and Walter Petrie in *Battle of Paris*

Suffering Sophie! That was Tucker (with Lila Lee) in *Honky Tonk*. Another strike-out.

Fanny Brice, of all people, suffered, too. She played the ugly duckling in *My Man*. Then it was back to Broadway where people saw Fanny to laugh.

Fanny Brice and Edna Murphy in *My Man*

John McCormack, one of the most beloved Irishmen since St. Patrick, took his turn in talkies, too, but somehow his movie box-office didn't create an overwhelming demand for a second McCormack film. The best-remembered thing about his *Song o' My Heart* was that it introduced a winsome colleen named Maureen O'Sullivan.

Ethel Waters torched a memorable "Am I Blue?" in *On With the Show*. But it was a long time before she'd be back on the screen in *Cabin in the Sky* and *The Member of the Wedding*.

Most fortunate of the unhappy ladies was Helen Morgan, who gave a remarkable performance as a blowsy burlesque queen in Rouben Mamoulian's striking *Applause*. But then Helen Morgan's forte was suffering — if only while she sat on top of a piano in a speakeasy and chanted her dirges to love.

Some newcomers to the movie medium managed very well after all. There was Jimmy, the well-dressed man — the Great Durante — who showed up in another Helen Morgan picture, *Roadhouse Nights*. Charlie Ruggles was in it, too.

Helen Kane's moment was fun while it lasted in things like *Dangerous Nan McGrew* and *Sweetie*, in which she boop-a-dooped her songs to Stuart Erwin.

Eddie Cantor was popular, too (though not in this corner), with his pop-eyed, frenetic cavorting. An early Cantor picture, *Palmy Days*, saw him teamed with Charlotte Greenwood, whose real movie career was to come years later in supporting comedy roles.

Queen High wasn't much of a movie and the ingénue who played with Charlie Ruggles and Stanley Smith really didn't cause much of a stir, but Ginger Rogers was to go on as quite the girl in later movie musicals.

Hardly a musical-comedy honey was this lady. Yet when Marlene growled "Falling in Love Again" in *The Blue Angel*, it *was* an

unforgettable movie musical moment. And
she was to have them many times again —
"You So-And So," "See What the Boys in the
Back Room Will Have," "Laziest Gal in
Town," "Ruins of Berlin," "Black Market,"
to list a few.

The Love Parade

And who would have ever thought that Jeanette MacDonald would become the queen of screen operetta, even though she decorated those early frothy Lubitsch musicals so well. In those days, Jeanette was always emerging from bed or about to step into a bath as she sang. The lady-in-waiting at her left is Virginia Bruce.

By far the biggest star to come to the early movie musicals was Maurice Chevalier. The idol of the Paris music halls, Chevalier's breezy insouciance and zat Gallic charm were just right for the sophisticated comedies with songs that were his trademark. Most of them were deftly directed by Ernst Lubitsch and among the still remembered Chevalier songs from films, you can list "Louise," "My Ideal," "The Love Parade," "You Brought a New Kind of Love To Me," and "One Hour With You."

Maurice Chevalier in *Paramount on Parade*

Jeanette MacDonald and Maurice Chevalier in *The Love Parade*

Long before she dreamed of duets with Nelson Eddy, Jeanette MacDonald had turned out to be the perfect teammate for Chevalier. It's hard to remember the MacDonald of that era without Chevalier, except for such an individual moment as her singing of "Beyond the Blue Horizon" with train wheels chugging in rhythmic accompaniment. Although they usually sparkled together in Lubitsch filmusicals, their best one was by Rouben Mamoulian. This was *Love Me Tonight,* with its superb Rodgers and Hart score brilliantly integrated into the film.

Jeanette MacDonald and Maurice Chevalier in *Love Me Tonight*

Operetta invaded the movies first with Sigmund Romberg's tuneful *Desert Song*, in which John Boles, as the dashing Red Shadow, sang to Carlotta King. And there was Myrna Loy as the sinuous native dancer.

Romberg's music also brought together the thrilling voices (and less than thrilling screen personalities) of Grace Moore and Lawrence Tibbett. This time it was in *New Moon*.

Rudolf Friml's *Vagabond King* gave Jeanette MacDonald some time off from her Chevalier pictures. Dennis King was the Francois Villon.

Marilyn Miller, the darling of the theatre, tiptoed prettily through the movie version of one of her top stage hits, *Sally*.

But the movie musical was fading. Singing Vivienne Segal made no movie dent in operettas like *Viennese Nights*. Nor did her handsome leading man, Walter Pidgeon — at least, not in that pre-Greer Garson time.

If the moment had been right, it might have been Bernice Claire and Alexander Gray as the King and Queen of movie operetta instead of MacDonald and Eddy. But by the time they made their appearance in *No, No Nanette* and *Song of the Flame*, fickle movie fans were staying away from anything with song, and theatres were advertising "This is *not* a musical." It was the end of the first movie musical era, with only a couple of Chevalier and Cantor pictures to bridge the two-year gap before *Forty-Second Street* and *Flying Down to Rio* and Bing Crosby started Hollywood's second musical movie period.

Alexander Gray and Bernice Claire in *No, No Nanette*

Alexander Gray and Bernice Claire in *Song of the Flame*

Most Memorable Songs and Musical Performances of the Period

NOTE: These are completely personal choices. You may remember *My Mother's Eyes* with fondness but you'll look in vain for it here. Performers are noted when their performances of the mentioned song were particularly memorable. Only songs written directly for the screen are listed; songs from theatre or other sources are mentioned only if there was special distinction in their screen performance. These are listed in no order at all — of excellence, chronological, alphabetical, or otherwise.

"Mammy," (by Sam Lewis, Joe Young, and Walter Donaldson) and "Toot-Toot-Tootsie Goodbye" (by Gus Kahn, Ernie Erdman, and Dan Russo) as sung by Al Jolson in *The Jazz Singer*.

"The Wedding of the Painted Doll," "Broadway Melody," "You Were Meant for Me" (by Arthur Freed, Nacio Herb Brown) from *Broadway Melody*.

"I Want to Go Places and Do Things" (Leo Robin, Richard Whiting) as sung by Nancy Carroll in *Close Harmony*.

"True Blue Lou" (Sam Coslow, Robin, and Whiting) from *Dance of Life* as sung by Hal Skelly.

"Tiptoe Through the Tulips" and "Painting the Clouds With Sunshine" (Al Dubin, Joe Burke) from *Gold Diggers of Broadway*.

"Singin' in the Rain" (Freed, Brown) from *Hollywood Revue*.

"Louise" (Robin and Whiting) as sung by Maurice Chevalier in *Innocents of Paris*.

"Dream Lover," "My Love Parade," "March of the Grenadiers" (Clifford Grey, Victor Schertzinger) as sung by Chevalier, Jeanette MacDonald in *The Love Parade*.

"My Man" (Channing Pollock, Maurice Yvain), "I'm an Indian" (Blanche Merrill, Leo Edwards) as sung by Fanny Brice in *My Man*.

"Am I Blue?" (Grant Clarke and Harry Akst) as sung by Ethel Waters in *On With the Show*.

"Look for the Silver Lining" (by B. G. DeSylva, Jerome Kern) as sung and danced by Marilyn Miller in *Sally*.

"Li-Po-Li" (Al Bryan, Ed Ward) as sung by Nick Lukas, and danced by Myrna Loy in *Show of Shows*.

"Sonny Boy" (DeSylva, Brown, and Henderson), "There's a Rainbow Round My Shoulder" (by Billy Rose, Al Jolson, Dave Dreyer) as sung by Jolson in *The Singing Fool*.

"I Don't Want Your Kisses" (Fred Fisher, Martin Broones) from *So This is College*.

"Turn on the Heat," "Sunny Side Up," "If I Had a Talking Picture of You," and "I'm a Dreamer, Aren't We All" (DeSylva, Brown, and Henderson) from *Sunny Side Up*.

"My Sweeter Than Sweet," (by George Marion, Jr., Richard Whiting) as sung by Nancy Carroll and Stanley Smith and "He's So Unusual" (Al Lewis, Abner Silver, Al Sherman) as sung by Helen Kane in *Sweetie*.

"Jericho" (Robin, Richard Myers), "I'll Always Be in Love With You" (Bud Green, Sammy Stept) from *Syncopation*.

"When My Dreams Come True" (Irving Berlin) from *The Cocoanuts*.

"Coquette" (Berlin) from *Coquette*.

"My Song of the Nile" (Al Bryan, George W. Meyer) from *Drag*.

"How Am I to Know" (Dorothy Parker, Jack King) from *Dynamite*.

"Where Is That Song of Songs for Me" (Berlin) from *Lady of the Pavements*.

"Pagan Love Song" (Freed, Brown) as sung by Ramon Novarro in *The Pagan*.

"Precious Little Thing Called Love" (Lou Davis, J. Fred Coots) as sung by Nancy Carroll in *Shopworn Angel*.

"Love, Your Magic Spell Is Everywhere" (Elsie Janis, Edmund Goulding) as sung by Gloria Swanson in *The Trespasser*.

"Chant of the Jungle" (Freed, Brown) from *Untamed*.

"Weary River" (Clarke, Silvers) from *Weary River*.

"Hooray for Captain Spalding" (Bert Kalmar, Harry Ruby), sung by Groucho Marx in *Animal Crackers*.

"You Brought a New Kind of Love to Me" (Irving Kahal, Pierre Norman, Sammy Fain) as sung by Chevalier in *The Big Pond*.

"Happy Days Are Here Again" (Jack Yellen, Milton Agar) from *Chasing Rainbows*.

"Three Little Words" (Kalmar, Ruby) from *Check and Double Check*.

"I Love You So Much" (Kalmar, Ruby) from *The Cuckoos*.

"Kiss Waltz" (Al Dubin, Joe Burke) from *Dancing Sweeties*.

"Peach of a Pair" (George Marion, Jr., Richard Whiting) as sung by Nancy Carroll and Buddy Rogers in *Follow Through*.

"Sing You Sinners" as sung by Lillian Roth, "In My Little Hope Chest" as sung by Nancy Carroll (both by Sam Coslow, W. Frank Harling) in *Honey*.

"Never Swat a Fly" (DeSylva, Brown, Henderson) from *Just Imagine*.

"It Seems to Be Spring," "My Mad Moment," "Let's Go Native" (George Marion, Jr., Richard Whiting) from *Let's Go Native*.

"Should I?" "Woman in the Shoe" (Freed, Brown) from *Lord Byron of Broadway*.

"Go Home and Tell Your Mother" (Dorothy Fields, Jimmy McHugh) from *Love in the Rough*.

"Beyond the Blue Horizon" as sung by Jeanette MacDonald, and "Give Me a Moment Please" as sung by Jack Buchanan (both by Robin, Harling, Whiting) in *Monte Carlo*.

"Sweeping the Clouds Away" (Coslow), "All I Want Is Just One Girl" (Robin, Whiting) as sung by Chevalier; "Dancing to Save Your Sole" (L. Wolfe Gilbert, Abel Baer) as sung and danced by Nancy Carroll in *Paramount on Parade*.

"My Ideal" (Robin, Whiting, Newell Chase) as sung by Maurice Chevalier in *Playboy of Paris*.

"Puttin' on the Ritz" (Berlin), "There's Danger in Your Eyes, Cherie" (Harry Richman, Jack Meskill, Pete Wendling) as sung by Harry Richman in *Puttin' on the Ritz*.

"When I'm Looking at You" (Clifford Grey, Herbert Stothart), "White Dove" (Grey, Franz Lehar) as sung by Lawrence Tibbett in *Rogue Song*.

"My Future Just Passed" (George Marion, Jr., Richard Whiting) from *Safety in Numbers*.

"Crying for the Carolines" (Sam Lewis, Joe Young, Harry Warren) from *Spring Is Here*.

"Two Hearts in Waltz Time" (Joe Young, Robert Stolz) from *Two Hearts in Waltz Time*.

"Waltz Huguette" (Brian Hooker, Rudolph Friml) as sung by Lillian Roth in *The Vagabond King*.

"You Will Remember Vienna" (Oscar Hammerstein II, Sigmund Romberg) from *Viennese Nights*.

"Making Whoopee" and "My Baby Just Cares for me" (Gus Kahn, Walter Donaldson) as sung by Eddie Cantor in *Whoopee*.

"Falling in Love Again" (Sammy Lerner, Frederick Hollander) as sung by Marlene Dietrich in *The Blue Angel*.

"Romance" (Edgar Leslie, Walter Donaldson) as sung by J. Harold Murray in *Cameo Kirby*.

"The Moon Is Low" (Freed, Brown) from *Montana Moon*.

"What Am I Bid?" (Robin, Karl Hajos) as sung by Dietrich in *Morocco*.

"Just a Little Closer" (Howard Johnson, Joseph Meyer) from *Remote Control*.

"Blue Is the Night" (Fred Fisher) from *Their Own Desires*.

"Singing a Song to the Stars" (Johnson, Meyer) from *Way Out West*.

"When Your Lover Has Gone" (E. A. Swan) from *Blonde Crazy*.

"Cuban Love Song" (Fields, McHugh) from *Cuban Love Song*.

"Delishious," "Somebody From Somewhere" (George and Ira Gershwin) from *Delicious*.

"While Hearts Are Singing" (Clifford Grey, Oscar Strauss) from *Smiling Lieutenant*.

"Come to Me" (DeSylva, Brown, Henderson) from *Indiscreet*.

"Out of Nowhere" (Ed Heyman, Johnny Green), "Consolation" (Robin, Whiting) from *Dude Ranch*.

"How Long Will It Last" (Max Leif, Joseph Meyer) from *Possessed*.

"Reaching for the Moon" (Berlin) from *Reaching for the Moon*.

"Three's a Crowd" (Al Warren, Harry Dubin) from *Crooner*.

"Isn't It Romantic," "Mimi," "Love Me Tonight," "Lover," "The Sun of a Gun Is Nothing But a Tailor" (Richard Rodgers, Lorenz Hart) as sung by Chevalier, Jeanette MacDonald in *Love Me Tonight*.

"One Hour With You" (Robin, Strauss, Whiting) from *One Hour With You*.

"You So-and-So" (Robin, Coslow) as sung by Dietrich in *Blonde Venus*.

"Paradise" (Gordon Clifford, Nacio Herb Brown) from *A Woman Commands*.

"Today I Feel So Happy" (Paul Abraham, Desmond Carter, Frank Eyton) from *Sunshine Susie*.

CHAPTER TWO

The Forty-Second Street Special

WARNER BROTHERS had created many firsts in the musical movie world. They had started movies singing in the first place with Vitaphone and Jolson's paean to his "Mammy." The first movie operetta, *The Desert Song,* came from Warners. So did the first color musicals (*On With the Show* and *Gold Diggers of Broadway*), and one of the first all-star revues. But musical movies had become a thing of the past, and even Warners didn't make them any more.

Then, in early 1932, Warners filled a special train with stars

The "Remember My Forgotten Man" number, featuring Joan Blondell, from *Gold Diggers of 1933*

like Laura LaPlante and starlets like Bette Davis and sent it roaring across the country on an exploitation tour. The studio had something it thought worth promoting — and the "42nd Street Special" drew attention to it with its celebrity-filled train tour. Warners had made another musical.

Forty-Second Street brought them back with a bang. Vaguely based on the earlier *On With the Show*, it had a story that was dated even then. But it introduced a new element — song and dance numbers created by Busby Berkeley especially for movies, bursting far beyond the bounds of what could be done on a stage, even though the story line pretended that they were happening within the conventional proscenium.

There were new songs — good ones — by Harry Warren and Al Dubin; new personalities, like Ruby Keeler and Dick Powell, in addition to such old established names as Bebe Daniels and Warner Baxter; lots of bright supporting people like Ginger Rogers; and, above all, girls in abundance — all shown off by the Berkeley technique.

Forty-Second Street was an immediate sensation — and so were the films, made on the same formula, which followed. Musicals were in again.

Take a tenor — the most bland and aggressively boyish specimen this side of Buddy Rogers (or that side of Pat Boone). Take a tapper — blank-faced, flat-voiced, but a decorative object at which the tenor can direct his songs.

Dick Powell and Ruby Keeler in *Gold Diggers of 1933*

Powell and Keeler in *Flirtation Walk*

Sometimes Dick Powell is in uniform — Army, Navy, or Marine. Sometimes his sweetheart is Doris Weston or Jeanne Madden or even Priscilla Lane. But usually she's Ruby Keeler — and they're perennial sweet young things.

Take a tough guy — Pat O'Brien or Warner Baxter or even Jimmy Cagney. Put him in an unlikely situation. For example, roistering with Ruby in *Footlight Parade*.

James Cagney and Ruby Keeler in *Footlight Parade*

54

Aline MacMahon

Fill in with "fun" people — acid Aline MacMahon, bright-eyed Joan Blondell, silly Sterling Holloway, pompous Guy Kibbee, for some examples.

Joan Blondell, Sterling Holloway, and Guy Kibbee in *Gold Diggers of 1933*

Be sure you have plenty of glimpses of Toby Wing, the very epitome of those honeys who make all those Berkeley patterns.

Decorate with dazzling damsels — all picked and put through their paces by a man with staggering dance production ideas. He's Busby Berkeley.

Songs — mostly by Warren and Dubin — and good songs, too. Songs like "We're in the Money" with a gold-digging Ginger Rogers leading the chorus.

Gold Diggers of 1933

Una Merkel, Ruby Keeler, George E. Stone, Warner Baxter, and Ginger Rogers in *Forty-Second Street*

That was the formula for *Forty-Second Street* and all the similar films which followed. In *Forty-Second Street* Ruby shared a chorus line with cuties like Ginger and Una Merkel.

It had a typical "boy-meets-girl" confrontation between Miss K. and Mr. P.

It had that famous scene where star (Bebe Daniels) breaks leg, whereupon director (Warner Baxter) puts our Ruby into the star spot. (Bebe had George Brent for consolation.)

George Brent, Bebe Daniels, Ruby Keeler, Warner Baxter, and Clarence Nordstrom in *Forty-Second Street*

Warners was so happy with its picture that it filled a railroad train — "The 42nd Street Special" — with stars and starlets like Bette Davis, Laura LaPlante, Preston Foster, and others, and sent it touting and tooting across the country. Musicals were back with a bang.

Plots were never the high points of the Warners' musicals. What you remember are the songs and the wonderful Busby Berkeley production numbers like "By a Waterfall" — full of water and girls, girls, girls!

Footlight Parade

Joan Blondell and girls in *Gold Diggers of 1937*

Berkeley got his girls into all manner of intricate formations as with Joan Blondell and her military ladies.

Gold Diggers of 1937

Or Joan and Dick might be just one couple in a whole platoon of rocking-chair romancers.

You could never overlook the Dubin-Warren songs. For example, "Lullaby of Broadway" which Berkeley staged with Wini Shaw, Powell, and a hundred dancing boys and girls.

Even before the Warners' days, Berkeley had attracted attention with his handling of the Goldwyn Girls in the Eddie Cantor pictures. Note the blonde in the exact center of this group. Girl named Goddard. Paulette, that is.

Ruth Etting, at Cantor's right, was his leading lady in *Roman Scandals*. But the others were the Goldwyn Girls, a group that included the long-tressed lovely over his left shoulder. Yes, it's Lucille Ball.

"Petting in the Park" number from *Gold Diggers of 1933*

Busby Berkeley musical sequences always started with a curtain rising and ended with a theatre audience applauding. But where, outside of the flair of the Berkeley imagina-tion, was there a theatre which could have accommodated most of the vast song-and-dance spectacles he dreamed up? Berkeley trademarks — endless vistas of interminable

"Shadow Waltz" number from *Gold Diggers of 1933*

Forty-Second Street

numbers of chorines, usually dressed in as little as possible; formations photographed from above, with the girls becoming Catherine wheels, kaleidoscopes, and opening flowers, or holding up cards and joining together to become giant American flags, N.R.A. sym-

bols, or portraits of F.D.R.; fondness for bad taste and dirty jokes (as in the leering infant of "Petting in the Park" and much of "Shuffle Off to Buffalo") or sordid situations (the whores and hopheads of "Shanghai Lil," the fall from the skyscraper in "Lullaby of Broad-

"Shadow Waltz" number from *Gold Diggers of 1933*

way," the "Remember My Forgotten Man" episode); choruses sung endlessly, with variations, over and over again — are what you best remember from all of those films of the era.

Ruby Keeler and Lee Dixon in *Ready, Willing, and Able*

Ruby didn't do as well after she and Powell were parted, even though she tapped on a giant typewriter with Lee Dixon.

Dick, though, went on with other leading ladies for awhile, even to such an elegant and unexpected choice as the beauteous Madeleine Carroll. That was in *On the Avenue,* (made at Fox, not Warners). More smart and sophisticated than the Warners backstagers, *On the Avenue* boasted one of Irving Berlin's best movie scores.

Berkeley went to straight directorial work, too, and only occasionally were hints of his former musical extravaganzas to be seen again. One such, from *Ziegfeld Girl*, presented Lana Turner, Hedy Lamarr, and Judy Garland in the "Stepped Out of a Dream" number.

Powell's popularity in musicals continued into the late thirties, reinforced by his hosting chores on the "Hollywood Hotel" radio show, in which he used to greet such guests as Irving Berlin, Louella Parsons, Eddie Cantor, Alice Faye, and Fred MacMurray.

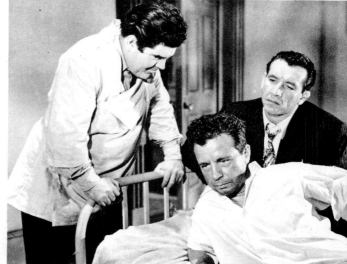

Stanley Andrews, Dick Powell, and Mike Mazurki in *Murder, My Sweet*

And one day a hardened Dick Powell turned up in a tough little melodrama, *Murder, My Sweet.* It was the end of the baby-faced tenor. It was the end of an era.

Most Memorable Songs
and Musical Performances of the Period

NOTE: The following songs are from pictures of the thirties which involved Powell, Keeler, Berkeley, and Warners. The note before the listing of songs at the end of Chapter One applies, as it does in all such song listings.

"Forty-Second Street," "Shuffle Off to Buffalo," "Young and Healthy," "You're Getting to Be a Habit With Me" (by Al Dubin, Harry Warren) as sung by Dick Powell, and Bebe Daniels in *Forty-Second Street*.

"By a Waterfall" (by Irving Kahal, Sammy Fain), "Shanghai Lil," "Honeymoon Hotel" (by Dubin, Warren) as sung by Powell, and James Cagney in *Footlight Parade*.

"We're in the Money," "I've Got to Sing a Torch Song," "Remember My Forgotten Man," "Pettin' in the Park," "Shadow Waltz" (by Dubin, Warren) as sung by Powell, Ginger Rogers, and Joan Blondell in *Gold Diggers of 1933*.

"Keep Young and Beautiful" as sung by Eddie Cantor, and "No More Love" as sung by Ruth Etting (both by Dubin, Warren) in *Roman Scandals*.

"I Only Have Eyes for You," "Dames" (by Dubin, Warren) as sung by Powell in *Dames*.

"Flirtation Walk," "Mr. and Mrs. Is the Name" (by Mort Dixon, Allie Wrubel) as sung by Powell in *Flirtation Walk*.

"Happiness Ahead," "Pop Goes Your Heart" (by Dixon, Wrubel) as sung by Powell in *Happiness Ahead*.

"Simple and Sweet" (by Kahal, Fain) from *Harold Teen*.

"I'll String Along With You" (by Dubin, Warren) as sung by Powell in *Twenty Million Sweethearts*.

"Going to Heaven on a Mule" as sung by Al Jolson; "Don't Say Goodnight," "Why Do I Dream Those Dreams?" and "Wonder Bar" as sung by Powell (all by Dubin, Warren) in *Wonder Bar*.

"Rose in Her Hair," "Lulu's Back in Town" (by Dubin, Warren) as sung by Powell in *Broadway Gondolier*.

"About a Quarter to Nine," "Latin From Manhattan" (by Dubin, Warren) as sung by Jolson in *Go Into Your Dance*.

"Lullaby of Broadway" (by Dubin, Warren) as sung by Wini Shaw in *Gold Diggers of 1935*.

"The Lady in Red" (by Dixon, Wrubel) as sung by Wini Shaw in *In Caliente*.

"Don't Give Up the Ship," "I'd Love to Take Orders From You" (by Dubin, Warren) as sung by Powell in *Shipmates Forever*.

"Where Am I?" as sung by Jane Froman, "September in the Rain" as sung by James Melton (both by Dubin, Warren) in *Stars Over Broadway*.

"Ev'ry Day" (by Kahal, Fain), "Fare Thee Well, Annabelle" (by Dixon, Wrubel) as sung by Rudy Vallee in *Sweet Music*.

"Thanks a Million," "Sitting High on a Hilltop" (by Gus Kahn, Arthur Johnston) as sung by Powell in *Thanks a Million*.

"I'll Sing You a Thousand Love Songs" (by Dubin, Warren) from *Cain and Mabel*.

"With Plenty of Money and You," "All's Fair in Love and War" (by Dubin, Warren) as sung by Powell in *Gold Diggers of 1937*.

"Through the Courtesy of Love" (by Jack Scholl, M. K. Jerome) from *Here Comes Carter*.

"Fancy Meeting You" (by E. Y. Harburg, Harold Arlen) as sung by Powell in *Stage Struck*.

"I'm Like a Fish Out of Water," "Hooray for Hollywood" (by Johnny Mercer, Richard Whiting) as sung by Powell in *Hollywood Hotel*.

"You're Laughing at Me," "The Girl on the Police Gazette," "I've Got My Love to Keep Me Warm" as sung by Dick Powell; "This Year's Kisses" as sung by Alice Faye; "Slumming on Park Avenue" as sung by Powell, Faye; (all by Irving Berlin) in *On The Avenue*.

"Remember Me" (by Dubin, Warren) as sung by Kenny Baker in *Mr. Dodd Takes the Air*.

" 'Cause My Baby Says it's So," "Song of the Marines," "You Can't Run Away From Love Tonight," "Night Over Shanghai," "The Lady Who Couldn't Be Kissed" (by Dubin, Warren, Johnny Mercer) as sung by Powell in *The Singing Marine*.

"Too Marvelous for Words" (by Mercer, Whiting) from *Ready, Willing and Able*.

"Ride, Tenderfoot, Ride" (by Mercer, Whiting) as sung by Powell in *Cowboy From Brooklyn*.

"Girl Friend of the Whirling Dervish," "Garden of the Moon," "Love Is Where You Find It" (by Mercer, Warren) from *Garden of the Moon*.

"Jeepers Creepers" (by Mercer, Warren) as sung by Powell in *Going Places*.

"You Must Have Been a Beautiful Baby" (by Mercer, Warren) as sung by Powell in *Hard to Get*.

Frank Sinatra and Bing Crosby in *High Society*

CHAPTER THREE

Crosby Comes to Croon

HE WAS Harry Lillis Crosby from Tacoma, Washington, but everybody called him "Bing." If you recognized the name at all, you knew him as one of the Rhythm Boys, who used to sing with Paul Whiteman's big band. He was the wild one, you'd hear.

And later, even though he was a little better established, there was a lot of pressure against his marrying Dixie Lee. Dixie was a rising starlet and her studio thought she should be involved with bigger game than the young crooner.

"Crooner" — that's what they called him. He had developed a singing style considerably different from that of the big-time singing stars of the day. He didn't shout like Jolson, nor was he lyrical like Morton Downey, and even Rudy Vallee was something else again. What Crosby did was pay attention to the melody and the lyrics, do some vocal tricks with "boo-boo-boo-boo's," and do it all with nonchalance and breeziness.

At first, they didn't take him seriously. But he caught on — oh, how he caught on — and soon you were hearing him on the radio and buying his records and seeing him in movie short subjects.

Finally, there was a feature movie, and the Crosby personality matched the Crosby voice. There were the *Big Broadcast* kind of movies and the *College Humor* kind...then a whole flock in which he got to sing a lot of wonderful songs and move easily through a forgettable plot with a forgettable leading lady in tow. And, of course, someone dreamed up the idea of sending him with Bob Hope and Dotty Lamour down a series of "Roads."

His movies got bigger and costlier and Crosby got more and more successful and popular. The Crosby stories began to get some substance, the Crosby co-stars began to have importance in their own right.

Crosby turned to drama, to characterization, and effortlessly conquered them, too. But his movies became fewer. Now, in his rare film appearances, he plays character roles.

But you can still see and hear him, looking not that much older, on a television show now and then. And there are all those years of Crosby movies turning up on your TV Late Shows.

Once he was just another member of a minor singing group which called themselves the Rhythm Boys and posed for gag pictures like this.

But then Bing Crosby moved, without his associates, into the radio world where his "boo-boo-boo" crooning style soon made him as much of a microphone name as were such contemporaries as Morton Downey and Kate Smith.

Crosby, Franklin Pangborn, and Irving Bacon

Movies came next — short Mack Sennett comedies through which Our Hero sauntered, crooning as he went.

And before you knew it, he was "A Star" — important enough to be caricatured.

Crosby and unidentified blonde in short comedy

Learn to Croon

SUNG BY
BING CROSBY
IN THE PARAMOUNT PICTURE
"COLLEGE HUMOR"

LYRIC BY
SAM COSLOW
MUSIC BY
ARTHUR JOHNSTON

Famous Music

Sheet music cover from *College Humor* with Mary Carlisle

A few years ago, Decca released a dozen or so long-playing record albums which detailed almost the entire movie career of Bing Crosby in song. And what songs they were — and are! The songs are what you remember about the Crosby musicals of the thirties, and the easy nonchalance of Bing himself, of course. But try to recall the sketchy plots of something like *Double or Nothing* or *Two for Tonight,* or just which of the anonymous and interchangeable leading ladies were which. They might be Mary Carlisle, Leila Hyams, or Judith Allen, or even Ida Lupino or Joan Bennett. Their only function was, decoration.

Usually there was a funny lady around to help out in those moments when Bing wasn't busy crooning to his "Mary" of the moment. But usually they didn't add much to the movies. One exception was Martha Raye, whose rowdy roughhouse was a contrast to the Crosby cool.

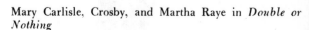

Mary Carlisle, Crosby, and Martha Raye in *Double or Nothing*

72

Ethel Merman and Crosby in *Anything Goes*

But mostly the funny ladies were as forgettable as the "Marys." Even Beatrice Lillie's "Double Damask Dinner Napkins" routine in *Doctor Rhythm* couldn't make her come to life in movies as the scintillating Bea of Broadway.

Nor did Ethel Merman make it in Crosby movies, even when she repeated her Broadway role in an inept film version of the Broadway hit *Anything Goes*, which inexplicably scuttled some of the great Cole Porter score to make way for some lackluster new songs.

Carlisle, Crosby, and Beatrice Lillie in *Doctor Rhythm*

73

Nor was Merman any more the dynamo Broadway knew in *We're Not Dressing*, although Carole Lombard had more personality than the usual "Mary." The movie, vaguely based on James M. Barrie's *Admirable Crichton*, had the usual good Crosby score and such comedy stalwarts of the era as Burns and Allen and Leon Errol.

One Crosby picture had a little more plot and characterization than most. This was *Sing You Sinners* which had the memorable "Small Fry" spot involving Fred MacMurray and an urchin named Donald O'Connor, who would eventually grow up to team à la Hope, Astaire, and Kaye with Crosby.

A later starter than Bing was the irrepressible Bob Hope. But eventually they found one another and started off on their "Road" .adventures. These usually involved at least one moment when the boys played "pattycake" as a preliminary to hauling off with a roundhouse attack on a hulking menace.

No "Mary" was Dotty. Lamour, usually clad in some seductive version of the famous sarong, joined the boys on all their trips down the various "Roads."

The lighthearted travels of the threesome might have gone on until they were old and gray. In fact, one of the final adventures had them wind up that way.

Lamour, Crosby, and Hope in *Road to Utopia*

But Bing kept getting into larger scale musicals, like *Holiday Inn,* in which there was necessity for only another "Mary" like Marjorie Reynolds, but not for a Dotty Lamour. Or he'd get tied up with other teammates. Fred Astaire, for example, or Danny Kaye, who joined him for *White Christmas,* in which, of course, Bing reprised his most famous song.

And finally the emphasis in the Crosby career changed — from lighthearted musicals to comedy-dramas with lots of warmth and with plenty of Oscar potential for the Bing. The first — and far away the best — of these was *Going My Way,* in which he was a happy-go-lucky Father O'Malley pitted against that darling, irascible oldster, Barry Fitzgerald.

Ingrid Bergman was darling, too, as the nice nun in the life of Father O'Malley in *Bells of St. Mary's.* But the sweetness was beginning to get a little sticky.

Bing went back to "big" musicals, like *Emperor Waltz* and *Connecticut Yankee,* but without particular success. Then came the turnabout — the intensely dramatic role of the drunken actor trying to make a comeback, with William Holden in *The Country Girl.*

But other dramas (like *Man on Fire*) didn't measure up, just as *Emperor Waltz*-style musicals hadn't. There was one more high-point appearance, in Cole Porter's *High Society,* with Sinatra, Grace Kelly, Celeste Holm, and, best of all, an exuberant Louis Armstrong.

In the war years, he frequently took time off to entertain the boys, along with such sidekicks as Hope and the young Sinatra. And, even though his movie stardom has waned, he remains very much a celebrity in his many off-camera appearances.

But it's sad to see a Crosby comeback in a stooge role such as the one he played in *Robin and the Seven Hoods* with Martin, Davis, Sinatra, and Bing's son, Philip, in other roles.

You may watch Crosby today doing a good character job in something like *Stagecoach*. But if you're like this writer, you'll be inclined to close your eyes and hear Crosby songs again — songs like "The Old Ox Road" sung by Bing, even with someone else on the screen.

The "Old Ox Road" number from Crosby's *College Humor* (with Mary Kornman and Jack Oakie)

Crosby and Joan Bennett in *Mississippi*

Of the many Crosbys, from Father O'Malley to star of *The Country Girl* to traveler down the various *Roads,* this writer will continue to treasure the first Bing, the breezy troubadour, who filled all those silly little movies with all of those unforgettable songs.

Crosby in *Rhythm on the Range*

The Bing Crosby Songs

THE FOLLOWING list of songs from Bing Crosby movies represents the best remembered, as well as my personal favorites, from his scores. Previous to his stardom in feature films, he appeared in several short comedies in which he sang such songs as "I Surrender, Dear," "Just One More Chance," "Out of Nowhere," and "Where the Blue of the Night Meets the Gold of the Day." The songs from shorts are not covered here nor are those not composed directly for the screen. When songs from a Crosby film were importantly performed by someone else in the picture, the other performer's name is listed. Otherwise, it's all Bing.

"Please," "Here Lies Love" (Leo Robin, Ralph Rainger) from *The Big Broadcast.*

"Learn to Croon," "Down the Old Ox Road," "Moon Struck" (Sam Coslow, Arthur Johnston) from *College Humor.*

"Temptation," "After Sundown," "Our Big Love Scene," "We'll Make Hay" (Arthur Freed, Nacio Herb Brown) from *Going Hollywood.*

"Thanks," "The Day You Came Along," "Black Moonlight" (Coslow, Johnston) from *Too Much Harmony.*

"June in January," "With Every Breath I Take" (Robin, Rainger); "Love Is Just Around the Corner" (Robin, Lewis Gensler) from *Here Is My Heart.*

"Love in Bloom" (Robin, Rainger) from *She Loves Me Not.*

"May I?," "Love Thy Neighbor," "Once in a Blue Moon," "Goodnight, Lovely Little Lady," "She Reminds Me of You" (Mack Gordon, Harry Revel) from *We're Not Dressing.*

"Why Dream?" (Robin, Rainger, Richard Whiting), "I Wished on the Moon" (Rainger, Dorothy Parker) from *The Big Broadcast of 1936.*

"Soon," "Easy to Remember," "Down by the River" (Richard Rodgers, Lorenz Hart) from *Mississippi.*

"Without a Word of Warning," "I Wish I Were Aladdin," "From the Top of Your Head to the Tip of Your Toes," "Takes Two to Make a Bargain" (Gordon, Revel) from *Two for Tonight.*

"Pennies From Heaven," "One, Two, Button My Shoe," "So Do I" (Johnny Burke, Arthur Johnston) from *Pennies From Heaven.*

"I Can't Escape From You" (Robin, Whiting), "Empty Saddles" (Billy Hill), "I'm an Old Cowhand" (Johnny Mercer); "Mr. Paganini" (Sam Coslow) sung by Martha Raye in *Rhythm on the Range.*

"Smarty" (Arthur Freed, Burton Lane); "All You Want to Do Is Dance," "The Moon Got in My Eyes," "It's the Natural Thing to Do" (Burke, Johnston); "After You" (Al Siegel, Sam Coslow), sung by Martha Raye, Frances Faye, in *Double or Nothing.*

"Blue Hawaii," "Sweet Is the Word for You" (Robin, Rainger), "Sweet Leilani" (Harry Owens) from *Waikiki Wedding.*

"This Is My Night to Dream," "My Heart Is Taking Lessons," "On the Sentimental Side" (Burke, Jimmy Monaco) from *Doctor Rhythm.*

"Pocketful of Dreams," "Don't Let That Moon Get Away" (Burke, Monaco); "Small Fry" (Frank Loesser, Hoagy Carmichael) from *Sing You Sinners.*

"East Side of Heaven" (Burke, Monaco) from *East Side of Heaven.*

"Funny Old Hills," "Sweet Little Headache," "I Have Eyes," "Joobalai" (Robin, Rainger) from *Paris Honeymoon.*

"A Man and His Dream," "An Apple for the Teacher," "Go Fly a Kite" (Burke, Monaco) from *The Star Maker.*

"Too Romantic" (Burke, Monaco) from *Road to Singapore.*

"April Played the Fiddle" (Burke, Monaco) from *If I Had My Way.*

"Only Forever," "That's for Me," "Ain't It a Shame About Mame" (Burke, Monaco) from *Rhythm on the River.*

"The Waiter, the Porter, and the Upstairs Maid" (Johnny Mercer), also performed by Mary Martin, Jack Teagarden in *Birth of the Blues.* (Note: This picture also featured an electrifying rendition of "St. Louis Blues" [W. C. Handy] by Ruby Elzy.)

"It's Always You," "You Lucky People You" (Burke, Jimmy Van Heusen) from *Road to Zanzibar.*

"White Christmas," "Be Careful, It's My Heart," "You're Easy to Dance With," "I'll Capture Your Heart," "Happy Holiday," "Abraham" (Irving Berlin), also performed by Fred Astaire in *White Christmas*.

"Moonlight Becomes You" (Burke, Van Heusen) from *Road to Morocco*.

"Sunday, Monday, and Always," "If You Please" (Burke, Van Heusen) from *Dixie*.

"Swinging on a Star," "Going My Way" (Burke, Van Heusen) from *Going My Way*.

"Ac-cent-chu-ate the Positive" (Johnny Mercer, Harold Arlen) from *Here Come the Waves*.

"Personality" (Burke, Van Heusen) from *Road to Utopia*.

"You Keep Coming Back Like a Song," "A Couple of Song and Dance Men" (Irving Berlin) from *Blue Skies* (also with Fred Astaire).

"But Beautiful" (Burke, Van Heusen) from *Road to Rio*.

"In the Cool, Cool, Cool of the Evening" (Mercer, Carmichael) from *Here Comes the Groom*.

"Tallahassee" (Frank Loesser) from *Variety Girl*.

"Out of This World" (Johnny Mercer, Harold Arlen) from *Out of This World*.

"Sunshine Cake" (Van Heusen, Burke) from *Riding High*.

"Life Is So Peculiar," "Accidents Will Happen" (Burke, Van Heusen) from *Mr. Music*.

"Once and For Always" (Burke, Van Heusen) from *A Connecticut Yankee in King Arthur's Court*.

"True Love," "I Love You, Samantha," "Now You Has Jazz" (Cole Porter), latter sung with Louis Armstrong in *High Society*.

"The Second Time Around" (Van Heusen, Sammy Cahn) from *High Time*.

Ginger Rogers and Fred Astaire in *The Barkleys of Broadway*

CHAPTER FOUR

Enter Dancing — It's Astaire!

FRED ASTAIRE was one of the most dazzling talents who ever flashed through Broadway. But to Hollywood he was just that unimpressive bony-faced type with large ears "who dances a little" — not to be taken seriously. He "danced a little" with La Belle Crawford herself, and didn't set the screen on fire, in *Dancing Lady*.

Then he was thrown into a subordinate role opposite a girl who usually played chorus dolls — Ginger Rogers. The picture was *Flying Down to Rio,* and you win first prize if you can name the leads — which Fred and Ginger were definitely not. (For the record, it was Dolores Del Rio, Gene Raymond, and Raul Roulien.)

After that, it was clear sailing for Astaire and Rogers in all those dear, silly, thin-plotted, music-thick movies of the thirties.

Then Ginger became An Actress and went on to "bigger," but not necessarily better, things. Fred, though, kept leaping like a gazelle through movie after movie — with Garland and Goddard, Hayworth and Hutton, Eleanor Powell and Jane Powell, Cyd Charisse, Joan Leslie, Vera-Ellen, and more. And eventually he was dancing with Leslie Caron and Audrey Hepburn. And finally nobody.

Oh, Astaire does a dance or two on TV once in a while, for old times sake, and he has played an occasional straight role. But it isn't what it used to be, is it? But then, what is? Presenting some glimpses of what it used to be —

A few months ago, New York television ran *Swing Time* for a week, two performances a night. There were people who timed it so they could tune in at the same time every showing to that magical moment when Fred Astaire went into one of the all-time top dancing sequences of movie musical history. This was "Bojangles of Harlem," and the perfection of Astaire's performance hasn't lessened.

Fred Astaire in *Swing Time*

Usually the tuners-in would stay also for "Waltz in Swing Time," one of the best Astaire dances with his most popular partner, Ginger Rogers. It seems to be the fashion now to sneer at Ginger's contributions. But she complemented him beautifully in those delights of the thirties — pretty and pert and with an appeal that had not yet developed into the relentless coyness of some of her later movies. Their tandem appearances were joys.

Astaire and Rogers in *Follow the Fleet*

Fred and Adele Astaire

But his first movie appearance created scarcely a ripple. The attention in *Dancing Lady* went to Joan Crawford in a rare musical movie role. Astaire was merely her almost-unidentifiable partner in an unexciting production number.

Of course, Astaire was already a darling of the theatre, dating back to the dancing days with his sister, Adele, and then with others, like Claire Luce, with whom he danced Cole Porter's throbbing "Night and Day" in *Gay Divorce*.

Joan Crawford and Astaire in *Dancing Lady*

He met Ginger and movie fame at the same time — when they played second leads in a Dolores Del Rio musical, *Flying Down to Rio.* When Ginger and Fred put heads together to join in the lively "Carioca," Del Rio was forgotten.

The typical Rogers and Astaire movie musical went something like this. Fred sees Ginger — Wham! But she usually thinks he's someone else, or misunderstands him somehow. So she's very haughty to him for most of the movie although she condescends to dance with him a couple of times. Funny folk like fussy Edward Everett Horton, sour-faced Helen Broderick, comedy valet Eric Blore, and comedy Lothario Erik Rhodes help complicate the situation. But the problem is always cleared up in the end in plenty of time for the most whirling Rogers and Astaire ballroom routine of all.

Top Hat

In *Carefree*

In *Shall We Dance*

Astaire brought elegance to the musical movie. Jaunty, unfailingly cheerful, he played all of his cardboard characters with tongue well in cheek, stopping frequently, praise Allah, to sing a song in his untrained, but

In *Top Hat*

In *Follow the Fleet*

In *Shall We Dance*

oddly insinuating, voice and, best of all, to dance. How to describe the impeccable style, the infinite variety, of his dancing. It's beyond the ability of this writer. But, oh, the joys! What high spots of movie musical history — the Fred Astaire dances!

In *The Story of Vernon and Irene Castle*

In *The Barkleys of Broadway*

In *The Story of Vernon and Irene Castle*

In *Top Hat*

Royal Wedding

The very top composers wrote their best scores for these movies. But if it wasn't Gershwin, it was Porter or Kern or Berlin. Ginger could give way to Hayworth or Audrey Hepburn or Leslie Caron. Horton and Broderick could be easily switched with someone like Victor Moore or Alice Brady. But the constant, the irreplaceable, the necessary ingredient was Fred Astaire. There just wasn't another one around.

Some time later, a very talented twosome — Gower and Marge Champion — had a few opportunities to bring the dance to the screen. But that was in the last days of movie musicals and they had no chance to become a latter-day Astaire-Rogers in popularity. Gower, though, would become one of Broadway's best directors.

Marge and Gower Champion in *Show Boat*

Astaire and Cyd Charisse in *Silk Stockings*

Astaire and Rita Hayworth in *You Were Never Lovelier*

When the Rogers-Astaire day was over and Ginger had gone on to straight, non-musical starring roles, Fred would continue on with other dancing damsels. It might be Eleanor Powell or Rita Hayworth, Judy Garland or Cyd Charisse. And eventually he would move right into the era, dominated by his only serious rival, Gene Kelly. But that's another story — the story of the "Golden Era" and the fall of the original movie musical. Astaire will come back to these pages again.

Astaire and Jane Powell in *Royal Wedding*

93

Astaire and Cyd Charisse in *The Band Wagon*

Astaire and Rita Hayworth in *You Were Never Lovelier*

Astaire, Eleanor Powell, and George Murphy in *Broadway Melody of 1940*

94

Gene Kelly and Astaire rehearsing "The Babbit and the Bromide" from *Ziegfeld Follies*

Astaire and Lucille Bremer in *Ziegfeld Follies*

Astaire and Kelly in *Ziegfeld Follies*

Leslie Caron and Fred Astaire in *Daddy Long Legs*

Astaire and Judy Garland in *Easter Parade*

96

Most Memorable Songs and
Dance Numbers from Fred Astaire Movies

NOTE: Unless otherwise noted, all the following musical numbers were sung, danced, or both, by Fred Astaire. Frequently he was joined in the numbers, most often by Miss Rogers, but also by other dancing ladies and such gentlemen as Bing Crosby. Songs from stage musicals or other sources, not composed directly for the screen are not included.

"My Dancing Lady" (by Dorothy Fields, Jimmy McHugh); "Everything I Have Is Yours" (by Harold Adamson, Burton Lane) from *Dancing Lady* (the songs here are memorable but, although Astaire made his screen debut dancing with Joan Crawford, the performances are forgotten).

"Carioca," as danced by Astaire and Rogers, "Orchids in the Moonlight," "Flying Down to Rio," "Music Makes Me" (by Gus Kahn, Edward Eliscu, Vincent Youmans) from *Flying Down to Rio.*

"The Continental," "Looking for a Needle in a Haystack" (by Herb Magidson, Con Conrad); "Don't Let It Bother You" (by Mack Gordon, Harry Revel) from *Gay Divorcee.*

"Lovely to Look At" (by Jerome Kern, Dorothy Fields, Jimmy McHugh) from *Roberta.*

"Cheek to Cheek," "Top Hat, White Tie, and Tails," "Isn't This a Lovely Day," "No Strings," "Piccolino" (by Irving Berlin) from *Top Hat.*

"I'm Putting All My Eggs in One Basket," "Let's Face the Music and Dance," "I'd Rather Lead a Band," "We Saw the Sea," "Let Yourself Go" as sung and danced by Astaire and Rogers; "Get Thee Behind Me, Satan" as sung by Harriet Hilliard (all by Irving Berlin) in *Follow the Fleet.*

"Bojangles of Harlem," "Waltz in Swing Time," "A Fine Romance," "The Way You Look Tonight," "Pick Yourself Up," "Never Gonna Dance" (by Dorothy Fields, Jerome Kern) from *Swing Time.*

"A Foggy Day in London," "Nice Work If You Can Get It," "Things Are Looking Up" (by George, Ira Gershwin) from *Damsel in Distress.*

"Slap That Bass," "Let's Call the Whole Thing Off," "They Can't Take That Away From Me," "They All Laughed," "Beginner's Luck," "Shall We Dance" (by George, Ira Gershwin) from *Shall We Dance.*

"Change Partners," "I Used to Be Color Blind," "The Night Is Filled With Music," "The Yam" (by Berlin) from *Carefree.*

"I Concentrate on You," "I've Got My Eyes on You" (by Cole Porter) from *Broadway Melody of 1940.*

"You Were Never Lovelier," "I'm Old Fashioned," "Dearly Beloved" (by Jerome Kern, Johnny Mercer) from *You Were Never Lovelier.*

"Shining Hour," "One for My Baby" (by Johnny Mercer, Harold Arlen) from *The Sky's the Limit.*

"Be Careful, It's My Heart," "You're Easy to Dance With," "White Christmas," "Happy Holiday," "I'll Capture Your Heart" (by Irving Berlin), most sung by Bing Crosby in *Holiday Inn.*

"You Keep Coming Back Like a Song," "A Couple of Song and Dance Men" (by Irving Berlin) from *Blue Skies.*

"This Heart of Mine" (by Arthur Freed, Harry Warren) danced with Lucille Bremer in *Ziegfeld Follies.*

"It Only Happens When I Dance With You," "Drum Crazy," "Stepping Out With My Baby," "We're a Couple of Swells," "A Fella With an Umbrella," "Better Luck Next Time," (by Irving Berlin) in *Easter Parade* (with Judy Garland, Ann Miller).

"I Left My Hat in Haiti," "How Could You Believe Me, etc.," "Too Late Now" (by Alan Jay Lerner, Burton Lane) from *Royal Wedding.*

"Something's Got to Give" (Johnny Mercer) from *Daddy Long Legs.*

"Bon Jour, Paris" (Roger Edens, Leonard Gershe) with Audrey Hepburn, Kay Thompson in *Funny Face.*

"That's Entertainment" (Arthur Schwartz, Howard Dietz) with Nanette Fabray in *The Band Wagon.*

CHAPTER FIVE

The Dancing Ladies

THEY ALL owed a great debt to Astaire — and later to Kelly. None of them — even the inimitable Eleanor Powell, or Britain's Jessie Matthews, or Cyd Charisse, or any of the rest — ever achieved the incomparable quality of these two.

Audrey Hepburn, Leslie Caron, Rita Hayworth, Shirley MacLaine — accomplished dancers all, yet they owe their screen celebrity to other talents.

But they, as well as such related performers as Sonja Henie and Esther Williams, had their place in musical movie history. Dance, then, all you ladies — dance, skate, or swim! The dancing ladies aren't around the movie world much anymore, but they certainly had their day.

Eleanor Powell and Ray Bolger in *Rosalie*

Eleanor Powell and Woody Herman's Orchestra in *Sensations*

Marilyn Miller tripped across the screen in a couple of early movie musicals. Ann Pennington was also a brief visitor in the late twenties. And there were others, right through the times of ladies like Ruby Keeler and Ginger Rogers. But the dynamo dancer on the distaff side of movie musicals was the long, lithe, leggy Eleanor Powell. The Powell pictures weren't much on plot; the Powell personality was no more than pleasant; the Powell acting ability considerably less than that. But the Powell dancing — that was something else — and you could count on at least a couple of tap spectaculars (frequently to some of the best Cole Porter) in every Powell picture.

Eleanor Powell in *Broadway Melody of 1936*

Eleanor Powell and George Murphy in *Broadway Melody of 1940*

99

Jessie Matthews and dance partner in *It's Love Again*

Powell's British counterpart was pert-faced, bright-eyed Jessie Matthews — "The Dancing Divinity" was her billing. From *It's Love Again, Evergreen,* and *First a Girl,* which were quite fun, to others which were quite awful, Jessie danced delightfully, sang prettily, and acted with some charm. Most Matthews plots involved her as a poor but honest girl who masqueraded as something else. America hoped that she would be brought to these shores to team with Fred Astaire. There was some such talk, but nothing ever came of it.

Jessie Matthews and Sonnie Hale in *First a Girl*

101

Rita Hayworth in *Cover Girl*

But Rita Hayworth did join Astaire. Although her eventual fame rested on her publicized image as America's "Love Goddess," she was also an accomplished dancer and some of her best pictures (*Cover Girl,* for instance, or *You Were Never Lovelier*) presented her this way, attractively teamed with such gentlemen as Messrs. Astaire and Gene Kelly.

Rita Hayworth and Fred Astaire in *You Were Never Lovelier*

Hayworth and Astaire in *You Were Never Lovelier*

Joan Crawford and dancers in *Torch Song*

Joan Crawford, as previously noted, introduced Astaire to the screen in *Dancing Lady*. But the cutie who had started her career as a Charleston queen and first became well known as one of "Our Dancing Daughters" became a "serious actress," so there were few jigs from the large-eyed lady in the years to follow. A "return" to this kind of role came in the late fifties with *Torch Song*, but it just confirmed her decision to stay with drama.

Fred Astaire and Joan Crawford in *Dancing Lady*

The Astaire-Rogers triumphs started some other teaming. Carole Lombard and George Raft did a sultry *Bolero* but a subsequent Lombard-Raft dance drama, *Rumba,* was a failure and they attempted no more.

103

Nancy Carroll had turned away from musicals, too. But with a run of poor films behind her, she attempted to revive her sagging career by putting on dancing shoes again. Her partner in *After the Dance* was George Murphy. They danced well but stole no thunder from Astaire and Rogers. It was just about the movie end for Nancy, although Murphy went on to dance again, before he eventually gave it up for the more strenuous whirl of politics.

Jean Harlow and dance partner in *Reckless*

Let's not call them "dancing ladies" but some of the others who would turn to a ballroom floor occasionally included such unexpected types as Barbara Stanwyck (in *Ten Cents a Dance*) and Jean Harlow (in *Reckless*). There were also Loretta Young (in *Men in Her Life*) and Margaret O'Brien (*Unfinished Dance*).

Barbara Stanwyck and players in *Ten Cents a Dance*

Vera-Ellen and Fred Astaire in *Three Little Words*

Other dancing girls who had their moment of glory — usually brief — in the movie musicals were Vera-Ellen, Sally Forrest, and Ann Miller. You could add Margo, Steffi Duna.

Sally Forrest and dancers in *The Strip*

Ann Miller in *Small Town Girl*

Gwen Verdon, as chorus girl, in *The Merry Widow*

One shapely redhead could be spotted occasionally in screen choruses. She was spotted much more identifiably when she left movies to step out on Broadway. Gwen Verdon's the name.

The terpsichorean talents of Cyd Charisse are almost equal to her beauty. She scored particularly in some of the better Gene Kelly efforts.

Cyd Charisse in *Black Tights*

Danny Kaye, Jeanmaire, and Farley Granger in *Hans Christian Andersen*

There may be a whole generation of movie fans who have never heard of Margot Fonteyn and other great dancers and who feel that Moira Shearer is the greatest ballerina of all time. Certainly the slim, redheaded beauty did more for ballet in films than any other woman. *Red Shoes* was a dazzling delight, and *Tales of Hoffman* was probably even more opulent, although a little too specialized for the tastes of the casual moviegoer.

A lively French import, Zizi Jeanmaire, came from ballet to enliven Danny Kaye's *Hans Christian Andersen*. But there have been only a couple of other screen roles — the ballet film, *Black Tights*, for instance — since then.

Moira Shearer in *Tales of Hoffman*

Moira Shearer in *Red Shoes*

In *Daddy Long Legs*

In *Gigi*

Much more successful as a screen personality was —and is — fragile, willowy Leslie Caron. With Kelly in *An American in Paris,* with Astaire in *Daddy Long Legs,* and joyously alone in *Lili* and *Gigi,* Caron made a distinct contribution to musical movies. Even so, she is more frequently seen these days in films without any music at all.

With Mel Ferrer in *Lili*

With Gene Kelly in *An American in Paris*

John Thomas, Lena Horne, and Archie Savage in *Broadway Rhythm*

The sexy seduction in Lena Horne's voice is what you remember. But Lena danced, too, and here's a *Broadway Rhythm* picture to prove it.

Audrey Hepburn and dancers in *Funny Face*

Juliet Prowse and Shirley MacLaine in *Can Can*

Two very well-established movie stars are occasionally reminded that they began as dancers. Shirley MacLaine dances well, but a picture like *Can Can* is no particular triumph although it got Juliet Prowse off and running. But Audrey Hepburn can point to her inspired antics in *Funny Face* as one of her real career high spots.

Carol Haney and dancers in *The Pajama Game*

Vera Zorina, Barrie Chase, and Carol Haney
are examples of girls whose very real dancing
talent didn't carry them very far on screen.

Sonja Henie in *Sun Valley Serenade*

Sonja Henie in *One in a Million*

Certainly there were non-dancers who made "dancing musicals." For what else were Sonja Henie's string of pale little program comedies, with their big moments of ice ballet?

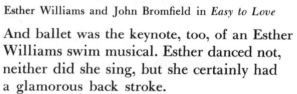

Esther Williams and John Bromfield in *Easy to Love*

And ballet was the keynote, too, of an Esther Williams swim musical. Esther danced not, neither did she sing, but she certainly had a glamorous back stroke.

Nelson Eddy and Jeanette MacDonald in *Bittersweet*

CHAPTER SIX

Make Love in Duets

OPERETTA HAD its innings in the first movie musical years, but when all screen musicals became anathema, those stagey ones with lush songs and ultra-romantic plots were the first to go. Bernice Claire and Alexander Gray, Vivienne Segal, Dennis King and the rest found themselves unwanted by Hollywood.

One, who had sparkled in Ernst Lubitsch-directed films with Maurice Chevalier, was Jeanette MacDonald. With song on screen washed up, she seemed on the verge of fading, too. She did a couple of routine comedies, but only because Lubitsch had authority enough to decide that he would reunite the two stars of his earlier pictures in another picture did she have a chance to return to musicals.

The Merry Widow was a success, and they decided to try one more operetta — a very old-fashioned type. It was unheralded, produced on a not-too-large budget, and featured an unknown singer named Nelson Eddy opposite Miss MacDonald. It was the beginning of a new bonanza.

Jeanette and Nelson sang their romances in a successful series and there were others to follow them — all the way from Irene Dunne and Allan Jones to Howard Keel and Kathryn Grayson. Opera stars like Lawrence Tibbett, Lily Pons and, especially, Grace Moore, came along with their high notes. But the patron saints of the period were MacDonald and Eddy.

Smart revues and TV shows now do take-offs on the kind of pictures MacDonald and Eddy used to make. But they were just right for the time, and it wasn't until they tried to move out of their own lacey Valentine world into something more chic and witty that the MacDonald-Eddy style of movies finally died out.

Clark Gable and Jeanette MacDonald in *San Francisco*

Jack Oakie, Kay Francis, and Jeanette MacDonald in *Let's Go Native*

Eddy and MacDonald in *Rose Marie*

Jeanette MacDonald and Nelson Eddy made love to music. Wrapped in each other's arms, face to face, they replaced kisses with cadenzas. They sang their sweet-sweet love stories on land and sea and in the Canadian Rockies. And if some critics were occasionally churlish about the quality of their voices and performances, the public paid no attention. For a half-dozen years, they were an institution. The public loved them. And Jeanette and Nelson sang — and sang — and sang!

If Eddy was virtually an unknown when they were first teamed, Jeanette was already a fading lady. She had weathered the first era of movie musicals (see Chapter One), most prominently in the delightful series of frothy tune-farces with Maurice Chevalier. But foolish little hodgepodges like *Let's Go Native* (with Jack Oakie, Kay Francis) had helped end the whole musical boom.

Only a couple of inconsequential MacDonald pictures came along in the next couple of years but then M-G-M took a chance on reuniting the Lubitsch-Chevalier-MacDonald trio for *The Merry Widow*. It was a lavish and stylish production and successful enough to encourage M-G-M to try another operetta.

Jeanette MacDonald and Maurice Chevalier in *The Merry Widow*

116

This was Victor Herbert's *Naughty Marietta,* crammed to the brim with lilting, tuneful, familiar songs. The book had its full quota of romantic foolishness — pirates, marching mercenaries, Casquette girls, masquerading princesses, and pleasant minor characters, including a bumbling Frank Morgan and a waspish Elsa Lanchester. It was all lots of fun and audiences adored it. Jeanette was a ravishing princess and Nelson Eddy her stalwart, if wooden, vis-a-vis.

In the next few years, they would be turning up together all over the map — literally from Broadway to heaven. In *Rose Marie,* it was the Pacific Northwest. He was a Mountie, she was an opera star, and they had their usual quota of misunderstandings (mostly over her brother and his prisoner — a very young James Stewart). But, of course, they came together in the usual way — "Indian Love Call" in this case.

New Moon. But the plots grew more inane, Jeanette's tiny temper tantrums became more kittenish, and her sweetness turned saccharine. Eddy never changed — personality minus. The innocent pleasure of their encounters grew tedious.

Romberg, Herbert, Friml, even Noël Coward — most of the "gems" of operetta found their way into the MacDonald-Eddy repertory. There were *Maytime* (above, the best after *Marietta*) and *Bittersweet, Sweethearts* and

Each sought occasional other movie mates. Jeanette was wooed by Clark Gable in *San Francisco,* and Allan Jones was only slightly more animated than Eddy (but sang impressively) in *The Firefly*.

Nor did Eddy's teaming with such ladies as Risë Stevens and Ilona Massey (above, in *Balalaika*) cause any major excitement.

Eddy even attempted a Dick Powell-type role in *Rosalie,* which was musical comedy rather than operetta. Eleanor Powell was his Keeler, but even though the film had some good Cole Porter songs, it was obvious that this kind of part wouldn't be Eddy's forte.

They made one more try at it — with a popular Rodgers and Hart musical comedy instead of the usual operetta. But *I Married an Angel* was carefully stripped of most of its wit and sophistication for the team. (Inez Cooper, Mona Maris, and an attractive newcomer, Janis Carter, were also involved.) It was the last of the MacDonald Eddy co-starrers.

With the beginning of the success of the MacDonald-Eddy movies, other operetta, and even some opera, appeared on the screen. Toward the end of the first movie musical era, one team with real voices appeared in a film operetta, *New Moon*. But there was no interest at all in Lawrence Tibbett and Grace Moore as a singing team.

Lawrence Tibbett and Grace Moore in *New Moon*

Inez Cooper, Mona Maris, Eddy, Janis Carter, and Jeanette MacDonald in *I Married an Angel*

Love Me Forever

Several years later, Grace Moore came back. This time — in spite of billing which insisted on "Miss Grace Moore" — they played down the "grand diva" aspects of her personality and did the best they could to make her just an apple-pie American girl. They even had her going into "Minnie the Moocher" in one picture. But some of them, especially *One Night of Love,* worked for her, and she had the voice and personality to make movie audiences sit still for arias.

Under Your Spell

122

And certainly Tibbett had the voice, too, in opera excerpts such as this from *Faust* in *Under Your Spell*. But he didn't have the physique, face, or flair — or the movies of any distinction — to make him as popular as was, briefly, Miss Moore.

Lupe Velez and Lawrence Tibbett in *Cuban Love Song*

Grace Moore and Tullio Carminati in *One Night of Love*

Risë Stevens and Nelson Eddy in *The Chocolate Soldier*   Grace Moore and Franchot Tone in *The King Steps Out*

Lily Pons in *I Dream Too Much*

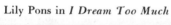

And still they came — the opera glamour girls. From Marion Talley to Risë Stevens, they made their movie or two and departed. Paramount's money was on Gladys Swarthout, and they gave *Champagne Waltz* a respectable production, with Fred MacMurray as leading man and Veloz and Yolanda to dance. But Gladys didn't come close to the Grace Moore peak.

Little Lily Pons tried, too. She was cute, her singing was thrilling, she had a good enough script, and the most promising new movie hero (Henry Fonda) as her first leading man. But *I Dream Too Much* was nothing special, her follow-up films even less.

Nino Martini's best movie, *The Gay Desperado,* was a wild and funny spoof, brilliantly made by Rouben Mamoulian. But somehow it didn't bowl over the box office and did nothing at all for the future movie career of Martini.

125

Determined to make a comeback, Gloria Swanson, still gorgeous and eager to show she could sing, latched on to the operetta cycle. Hers was a film version of Jerome Kern's *Music in the Air* with John Boles, Douglass Montgomery, and June Lang also on hand. It helped keep Gloria off the screen for another long spell.

The one major dramatic star who was successful with her occasional forays into film operetta was Irene Dunne. Dunne was almost always a Jerome Kern girl — in *Roberta, Sweet Adeline, High, Wide, and Handsome,* and others, and most notably, *Show Boat.* Here she and Allan Jones played out the story of Magnolia and Ravenal, with all the favorite songs.

Mario Lanza in *The Great Caruso*

Even bigger at the box office than Grace Moore — but for an even briefer period — was Mario Lanza. His voice was magnificent but his pictures were trivial, and reports of a monumental temperament, a monumental appetite, and a monumentally stormy private life helped kill the movie makers' interest.

Robert Sterling and Anne Jeffreys

Last of the movie singing twosomes of any particular note were Howard Keel and Kathryn Grayson — he personable, with a strong voice and more ease in his acting than most of his kind; she, pretty, chilly, and fond of doing prima donna trills. Together or separately, they contributed to such films as *Show Boat, Annie, Get Your Gun, Kismet, Seven Brides for Seven Brothers,* and *Kiss Me Kate.*

But the end of another musical movie era was at hand, and soon gone from movie screens were the Keels and the Graysons, as well as the Jane Powells, Ann Blyths, and Betty Huttons. Even someone like Anne Jeffreys, who had gone to Broadway to break away from routine movie roles and had made a name for herself as a musical-comedy queen, delayed too long in accepting offers that would have made her a movie musical star. For, soon, there were no movie musicals in which to appear. She and her husband, Robert Sterling, settled for supper clubs and TV.

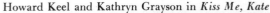

Howard Keel and Kathryn Grayson in *Kiss Me, Kate*

Shirley Temple in *Rebecca of Sunnybrook Farm*

CHAPTER SEVEN

Here Come the Kids

THEY DON'T seem to have child stars any more — even adolescents. Oh, occasionally a Hayley Mills will make a bit of a splash, or a Patty Duke, but mostly you'll find the kids in TV series, not in the movies.

Way back when, there were Jackie Coogan and Baby Peggy. Later, youngsters like Jackie Cooper came along. But the big-time baby of all time was Shirley Temple. She brought song to children's movies. And, following in her footsteps, came some other kids — including the pen-and-ink creations of Walt Disney.

And there were the adolescents — Deanna Durbin, Mickey Rooney, Donald O'Connor, and the rest. And, of course, Judy Garland.

They're all grown up now, and there hasn't been anyone around to take the place of any of them. But what happy days and what happy youngsters they all were (or seemed to be) — back there singing and dancing through the thirties and early forties.

"Who's Afraid of the Big, Bad Wolf!" sang Walt Disney's indestructible "Three Little Pigs," and their defiant tune became the theme song of the darkest thirties.

Standing for even more in these Depression days was, of all things, a little girl with floppy curls, misplaced dimples, and a piping voice. Shirley Temple usually had to go through all sorts of problem situations but she was true-blue and always came sunnily through. For Shirley was the perennial optimist, and the world was ready for optimism. From the moment in a tired little revue called *Stand Up and Cheer* that James Dunn sang "Baby Take a Bow" and "Baby" took her bow, Shirley Temple was in.

Let's face it, there were few unforgettable movie musical moments connected with Shirley Temple pictures — not "Animal Crackers in My Soup" or "On the Good Ship Lollypop" or any of the others. But one does remain in the memory — Shirley doing her little dance with the great Bill Robinson, cast in the stereotype "darkie" role given to all Negroes in those days. But there was no stereotype about Robinson as a personality or as a great dancing star.

The Little Colonel

As Shirley typified the swing away from Mae Wests and Jean Harlows, so, to an even greater degree, did Walt Disney and his movies. From Mickey Mouse and Silly Symphony to full-length cartoon movie magic was an unexpected step but Disney took it with *Snow White and the Seven Dwarfs*, which one critic called "the happiest event since the Armistice."

Pinocchio, Dumbo, Bambi, more — the Disney world was a delight. And, although many musical purists scorned it and much of the regular Disney audience stayed away, his *Fantasia*, on the whole, was a major step forward in presenting great music on the screen.

Mickey Mouse in *Fantasia*

Barbara Read, Deanna Durbin, and Nan Grey in *Three Smart Girls*

Deanna Durbin, Leopold Stokowski, and orchestra in *100 Men and a Girl*

With Shirley and Disney pointing the way, other studios found gold mines in singing youngsters. Universal, for instance, had been in big financial trouble but the films of one apple-cheeked adolescent helped bail them out. This was Deanna Durbin, whose high sweet voice and personality to match were well used in a series of bright, enjoyable little program pictures like *Mad About Music* and *Three Smart Girls*.

High spot for Deanna was *100 Men and a Girl* in which she sang with Leopold Stokowski. But, as she grew up, she began to fight a weight problem at the same time as her scripts grew slimmer. Finally, after a series of disappointing movies, she gave it all up, retired to France, and has resisted all attempts to draw her back into the entertainment world.

Of course, there were Judy and Mickey — and more of them anon — but there were other youngsters who had their moment in the movie musicals. These included Gloria Jean, Peggy Ryan, Susanna Foster, and the tiny soprano, Jane Powell. When Jane had her first "grown up" role in *A Date With Judy,* she shared scenes with another debutante. This one didn't sing — she didn't have to. Elizabeth Taylor!

Bobby Breen and Uilani Silva in *Hawaii Calls*

One little boy with a syrupy voice made a few of the most saccharine movies ever filmed. He was Bobby Breen.

But Donald O'Connor's natural talents came through strongly, first as the "Small Fry" of Bing Crosby's *Sing, You Sinners* and then, as he grew up, in such pictures as *Singin' in the Rain,* where he had to share scenes and match abilities with Gene Kelly. He could — and did.

Of course, Mickey Rooney could do just about anything and do it remarkably well. And nobody was more appreciative of his versatility, it would seem, than Mickey himself. Brashness was a part of his personality, but sometimes, you might feel, there was almost too much personality. Even so, he was lively and funny in his "Andy Hardy" days, when he was always surrounded by such members of the pretty young set as Ann Rutherford, Cecilia Parker, Lana Turner, and Judy Garland

Love Finds Andy Hardy

Broadway Melody of 1938

Strike Up the Band

He was even more frenetic in a series of movies he made with Judy, pictures like *Babes in Arms, Strike Up the Band, Girl Crazy, Babes on Broadway.* Here Mickey would sing, dance, do imitations, and play every instrument in the band. But he burned himself out before he was really grown up and, although he is still capable of extraordinary performances, the opportunities for them grow fewer.

The most rewarding, dazzling, and eventually heartbreaking career of any of the movie musical youngsters was that of Judy Garland. Judy of the button nose, the great dark eyes, the infectious giggle, the quavering, but full-bodied voice seemed just another nice little girl at first. Then she sat down and began to sing a love letter to "Dear Mr. Gable," and you knew this was something special.

Her film frolics with Mickey carried her along to a point where she was at least as popular as he and Deanna were. But then came pictures which lifted her to still another level.

Babes in Arms

The Wizard of Oz may well be, along with Disney's best, the most ideal entertainment for children ever produced by Hollywood. Here Judy was absolutely radiant as she joined three fabulous friends to follow the yellow brick road to find the wonderful, magical land that lay "somewhere over the rainbow." A salute, also, to Ray Bolger, Jack Haley, and the great Bert Lahr.

The happiness that was over Judy's rainbow was to prove elusive, but there was a time when everything seemed completely right and wonderful with Judy's career. Has there ever been a more joyous, more warming movie musical than Meet Me in St. Louis, with Vincente Minnelli affectionately re-creating Sally Benson's fondly remembered turn-of-the-century family chronicles? Has there ever been a more darling little sister than Margaret O'Brien's Tootie? Has there ever been anyone quite like Judy?

Just to prove that she was also very sensitive as a straight actress, Judy co-starred with Robert Walker in a lovely little picture, *The Clock*, in which there were no songs at all.

But mostly it was songs and sparkle — knocking herself out to entertain with such great entertainers as Rooney, Fred Astaire or, as in *The Pirate*, with Gene Kelly, extolling the merits of being a clown.

James Mason and Judy Garland

The ups-and-downs of the Garland career are too well known to dwell on here. The downs were dizzying, devastating to Judy and to her fans. There was the first return to glory — the great Garland triumph in *A Star Is Born*. But she didn't win a deserved Academy Award, and widely publicized production problems skyrocketed the cost of the picture. The descent began again.

James Mason, Judy Garland, and Charles Bickford

Judy does come back — again and again: the Palace in New York, the Palladium in London, the great concert tour that wound up on that never-to-be-forgotten night at Carnegie Hall.

But Judy seems to be a yo-yo — for every up there's a down. Her eagerly awaited television series, even with guests like Martin and Sinatra, failed miserably. So did movie returns in *A Child Is Waiting* and *I Could Go on Singing*.

Yet, even at lowest ebb, Judy is nothing less than one of the great stars we have produced. And now there's another — Liza Minnelli, her daughter — and she might just carry on the tradition. But, as Liza goes forward, don't count Mama out. There's always another triumph left in Judy Garland.

139

CHAPTER EIGHT

Bring on the Blondes

Marlene Dietrich

Mae West

There'll always be a blonde in the musical movies. From the pre-Astaire Ginger Rogers to the post-Rodgers Shirley Jones, from Alice Faye to Doris Day, from Betty Grable to Betty Hutton, even to these two ladies who were really not of musical movies at all. There generally came a time when Marlene purred a throaty ditty, or when Mae West undulated across the screen, not quite singing, not quite speaking, paeans to her particular world of sex and men. And these "musical" moments were always high spots of any West or Dietrich movie.

But when you spoke of "blondes in movie musicals," you generally referred to these two. When they came together in *Tin Pan Alley* as favorites of Sultan Billy Gilbert, Alice Faye was still a big name, Betty Grable just a rising one. But soon, Betty was to replace Alice as the Number One movie musical blonde.

Frances Langford, Patsy Kelly, George Raft, and Alice Faye in *Every Night at Eight*

Faye's heyday was the thirties and early forties. Starting out as a platinum blonde who seemed to be almost caricaturing Jean Harlow (as Mansfield was later to caricature Monroe), she eventually softened her appearance, her voice, and her personality. Although such elaborate epics as *In Old Chicago* and *Alexander's Ragtime Band* were her "big" pictures, her best ones were a series of topical, brightly written, tuneful programmers like *Sing, Baby, Sing* and *Wake Up and Live*. Many teamed her with the perennially smiling Don Ameche, but in the big budget jobs, Ameche smiled though

Alice Faye and James Dunn in *George White's Scandals*

Alice Faye and Tony Martin in *You Can't Have Everything*

Tyrone Power, Alice Faye, and Don Ameche in *In Old Chicago*

Alice Faye and Jack Haley in *Wake Up and Live*

his heart was breaking. Because here, you see, it was a foregone conclusion that Alice would wind up with Tyrone Power and Don would be relegated to the position of faith-

ful, long-suffering friend. You were likely to see people like Joan Davis and the Ritz Brothers around, too, and, for some, that was hardly a blessing. But Alice sang energeti-

Edward Arnold, Don Ameche, Alice Faye, Henry Fonda, and Warren William in *Lillian Russell*

Alice Faye and Pamela Tiffin in *State Fair*

Jack Oakie, Alice Faye, and John Payne in *Hello, Frisco, Hello*

cally and if her acting technique was largely limited to a chubby-cheeked grin or a heavy-lipped pout, it didn't really matter. Many of her movies were pleasant diversions.

Jack Haley, Alice Faye, Don Ameche, Tyrone Power, and others in *Alexander's Ragtime Band*

Lucille Ball, Harriet Hilliard, and Betty Grable in *Follow the Fleet*

Betty Grable and Hermes Pan in *Moon Over Miami*

Betty Grable's pictures were even thinner than Faye's because, in the wartime years in which she flourished, there was no attempt to interject even the mild touches of topical satire that had marked those of her studio in the thirties. They were almost all of such a sameness that only by changes of costumes

Betty Grable, Joe Penner, and Frances Langford in *Collegiate*

Bert Wheeler, Betty Grable, and Robert Woolsey in *Hips, Hips Hooray*

and leading men — John Payne instead of Victor Mature or Dan Dailey — could you tell them apart. People like Phil Silvers or Carmen Miranda or Charlotte Greenwood were likely to turn up and they were welcome. But mostly Grable movies were for Grable. She sang and danced well enough to get by

Dan Dailey and Betty Grable in *Mother Wore Tights*

Betty Grable in *Down Argentine Way*

147

Betty Grable and Jane Wyman in *Footlight Serenade*

(she had had enough experience all through the thirties as ingénue with the likes of Wheeler and Woolsey in lots of obscure tune films). But you went to Betty Grable movies to look at Betty Grable — the girl drawn by Mr. Petty come to life — the Pin-Up Girl herself!

Betty Grable, Dan Dailey, and dancer in *My Blue Heaven*

Ginger Rogers and Jack Oakie in *Sitting Pretty*

Ginger Rogers and dancers in *Lady in the Dark*

Ginger Rogers was a pert and perky blonde honey in musicals like *Sitting Pretty* before she ever heard of Fred Astaire. In her post-Astaire era, however, she had become "an actress" so there had to be a pretty weighty reason for her to get back into dancing shoes. One such weighty reason was the crashingly dull film version of the Moss Hart-Kurt Weill play *Lady in the Dark,* which with Gertrude Lawrence, had been rather a sprightly show.

Priscilla Lane and Dick Powell in *Cowboy from Brooklyn*

Priscilla Lane was another bubbling blonde who was handy to have around as a foil to the likes of Dick Powell in the thirties.

June Allyson was cute as a button in *Two Girls and a Sailor* in which Gloria DeHaven and Jimmy Durante were pretty cute, too. But subsequent films saw Junie getting "cuter" and "cuter" ad nauseam.

Ben Blue, Red Skelton, Rags Ragland, and Ann Sothern in *Panama Hattie*

And Ann Sothern did some fluffy little things which led to her doing *Panama Hattie*. But Annie was no Merman.

Jimmy Durante, Gloria DeHaven, and June Allyson in *Two Girls and a Sailor*

150

Bob Fosse, Janet Leigh, Betty Garrett, and Tommy Rall in *My Sister Eileen*

Certainly nobody physically fitted the idea of pretty lady of the "tuners" better than did Janet Leigh. But her few films of this type were poor enough that she turned to stronger things — like being stabbed in the *Psycho* shower.

One of the most talented girls in the business is Mitzi Gaynor. But, in spite of pulling the prize plum of the Nellie Forbush role in *South Pacific* right from under the noses of Doris Day and others who were suggested, her movie career never quite caught on.

Mitzi Gaynor and Ray Walston in *South Pacific*

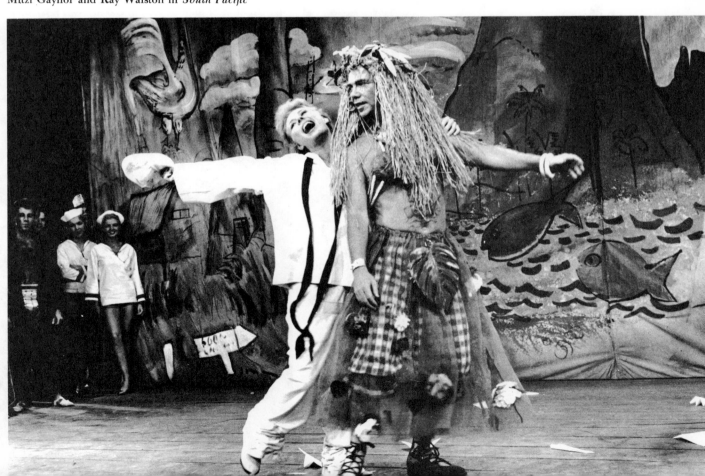

Marilyn Monroe and Jane Russell in *Gentlemen Prefer Blondes*

Marilyn Monroe and dancers, in *Gentlemen Prefer Blondes*

Marilyn was something else. She didn't dance very well and her singing was almost a take-off on Helen Kane. But a couple of her very best pictures were musicals (*Some Like It Hot, Gentlemen Prefer Blondes*) and who cared if she wasn't really up to the song-and-dance spots?

152

Marilyn Monroe, Donald O'Connor, and Mitzi Gaynor in *There's No Business Like Show Business*

Marilyn Monroe in *There's No Business Like Show Business*

153

Betty Hutton in *Annie Get Your Gun*

Howard Keel, Jane Powell in *Seven Brides for Seven Brothers*

Most boisterous blonde of the musical movies, Betty Hutton caterwauled through a number of routine jobs (her best picture, *Miracle of Morgan's Creek,* had nary a song) before getting her best song role in *Annie Get Your Gun.* Strangely, this high point in her career was her last film of any consequence.

Jane Powell, too, faded fast after her best movie, *Seven Brides for Seven Brothers.* She had been a sort of latter-day Deanna Durbin as an adolescent and still is something of a draw in nightclubs and summer theatre. But she grew up at the time that musical movies were being shelved.

Shirley Jones was Laurie in *Oklahoma* and Julie in *Carousel,* which should have been quite a parlay for any star. But she didn't make news until she played a non-singing supporting role in *Elmer Gantry.*

Shirley Jones, Gordon MacRae in *Carousel*

Vivian Blaine in *Guys and Dolls*

Sheree North

After the days of Faye and Grable, Fox tried with others — Vera-Ellen, June Haver, Sheree North, for instance — but without success. Another who missed was Vivian Blaine. But for Blaine there was Broadway and the unforgettable Adelaide of *Guys and Dolls,* a role she reprised satisfactorily in the not-too-satisfying screen version.

Vera-Ellen, June Haver, and Vivian Blaine in *Three Little Girls in Blue*

Dorothy Dell was a beauty from the *Follies* who was starting to come along in movies like *Little Miss Marker* with Shirley Temple. If you heard her sing "With My Eyes Wide Open, I'm Dreaming" in *Shoot the Works*, you haven't forgotten her. But an automobile accident ended her life just as she was on the threshold of fame.

We'll always remember the dark-haired, dark-eyed Frances Langford of the "Mood for Love"-"Easy to Love" song days. But for most of her movie years, Frances was a blonde, as was such another distinct brunette, Dinah Shore.

Peggy Lee is one of the really great stars of the record-nightclub world. But her screen career was brief and unimpressive except for one moving scene in *Pete Kelly's Blues,* a scene which had nothing to do with song.

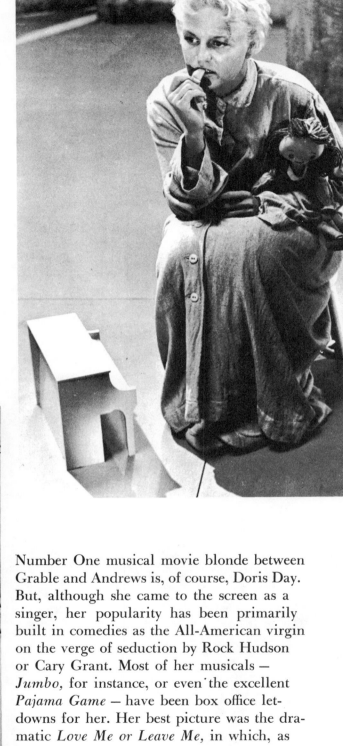

Number One musical movie blonde between Grable and Andrews is, of course, Doris Day. But, although she came to the screen as a singer, her popularity has been primarily built in comedies as the All-American virgin on the verge of seduction by Rock Hudson or Cary Grant. Most of her musicals — *Jumbo,* for instance, or even the excellent *Pajama Game* — have been box office letdowns for her. Her best picture was the dramatic *Love Me or Leave Me,* in which, as Ruth Etting, she sang, too.

Doris Day and John Raitt in *The Pajama Game*

CHAPTER NINE

The Golden Era

Gene Kelly and Frank Sinatra in *Anchors Aweigh*

The "Golden Era" of original movie musicals began approximately in the mid-forties and fizzled out some ten years later. M-G-M was the studio most involved, although there were some worthy entrants from others, too. Among the names that leap immediately to mind as representative are producer Arthur Freed, directors Vincente Minnelli and Stanley Donen, writers like Betty Comden and Adolph Green, composers like Lerner and Loewe, stars like Astaire and Judy Garland, Sinatra, and Leslie Caron. And, first and foremost, symbolizing the whole happy-go-lucky flash and dash of the period, a lean, casual, black-Irishman with a crooked grin, a throaty voice, and a pair of the happiest feet in history.

Gene Kelly in *An American in Paris*

Gene Kelly, fresh from Broadway's *Pal Joey*, first danced on the screen as a partner to Judy Garland, herself an early representative of the best days of original movie musicals with *Meet Me in St. Louis* and others that were to follow. Their picture, *For Me and My Gal,* was one of those thoroughly conventional items about the ups and downs of a vaudeville team, but it established Kelly immediately as one of the most arresting personalities.

159

Gene Kelly in *Cover Girl*

Most of Rita Hayworth's pictures projected the steamy image of "the love goddess." One notable exception was *Cover Girl* in which her very definite talent as a dancer was displayed. And again we had Gene Kelly, dancing, both with Miss Hayworth and alone, in the extraordinary "Alter Ego" number.

Gene Kelly, Rita Hayworth, and Phil Silvers in *Cover Girl*

Kelly and Frank Sinatra in *Anchors Aweigh*

Claire Sombert and Gene Kelly in *Invitation to the Dance*

As Kelly progressed in screen stature, he brought new thrill to movie dancing. He was versatile — Kelly would tackle just about everything from classical ballet to the buck and wing; original — his dance numbers, mostly conceived and choreographed by himself, were consistently fresh and unhackneyed; individual — his style was all his, hard-driving, athletic, acrobatic. You could never mistake Gene Kelly's dancing for that of anyone else. He has constantly proclaimed his debt — and, indeed, the debt of all movie musicals — to Astaire. But, having acknowledged Astaire's leadership in the art of screen dance, Kelly took off into his own world — a very different world of the dance from that of the precise, delicate, humorous Mr. A.

Fred Kelly and Gene Kelly in *Deep in My Heart*

161

Gene Kelly in *Anchors Aweigh*

Gene Kelly and Fred Astaire in *Ziegfeld Follies*

Kelly and Vera-Ellen in *On the Town*

He and Astaire worked together in one film only, a Gershwin song-and-dance comedy spot, "The Babbit and the Bromide," in *The Ziegfeld Follies*. It was pleasant to watch but taxed neither star.

On his own, Kelly burst forth in one stunning screen musical after another. Even his performance as D'Artagnan in the non-musical *Three Musketeers* seemed choreographed with its leaps and duels. And even such an inferior picture as *Summer Stock* would have its memorable moment — in this case, the dance with the newspaper on the squeaky board.

His *Invitation to the Dance* was a box-office failure but an important screen experiment. His contributions to such all-star musicals as *Words and Music* (a Kelly-choreographed "Slaughter on Tenth Avenue") or *Deep in My Heart* (a lively comedy routine performed with his own brother, Fred) were big moments in bad pictures.

162

Kelly and Leslie Caron in *An American in Paris*

But mostly the Kelly pictures were good-better-best — among the very tops in all movie musical history. There were the rollicking *Anchors Aweigh* and a mad romp *On the Town*, practically an original as a movie in spite of the stage show which had preceded it. Sinatra backstopped him well in both of these.

There were *The Pirate* and *Les Girls*, both with Cole Porter scores and inventive dance spots.

There was the dazzling *An American in Paris* with a Gershwin score and with a lissome Leslie Caron along to help in some of the most ambitious, and successful, dance sequences from any Kelly film. These included the extended, electrifying title ballet with its decor derived from Utrillo, Renoir, Lautrec, Dufy, and Rousseau.

It's Always Fair Weather came late in the cycle. Musicals were already dying at the box office and this failed, too. But it was a good one.

Taina Elg, Mitzi Gaynor, Kay Kendall, and Kelly in *Les Girls*

Best of all was *Singin' in the Rain* — this department's choice as the best movie musical ever made. The inspiration for the bright and witty book of Betty Comden and Adolph Green was the "Once in a Lifetime" era when movies were beginning to talk. Arthur Freed's production opened the catalogue of songs he had written with Nacio Herb Brown, perfectly chosen for the period. Kelly (who also co-directed with Stanley Donen) has

never been more deft and engaging, never has he displayed such exuberant verve and flair. Donald O'Connor was a particularly competent teammate, Debbie Reynolds was a vivacious leading lady, Cyd Charisse helped a great deal with the dancing, and Jean Hagen slammed across a wickedly funny movie-star caricature. Everything about *Singin' in the Rain* worked just a little better than it has in any movie musical before or since.

Bing Crosby and Fred Astaire in *Blue Skies*

Kay Thompson, Astaire, and Audrey Hepburn in *Funny Face*

The Old Master, Fred Astaire himself, was very much a part of this "Golden Era." There were such pleasant affairs as *Easter Parade* and *Royal Wedding*, *The Barkleys of Broad-* *way*, *Blue Skies*, and *Daddy Long Legs.* And there were the two brilliant films which capped his career as a great musical star, *The Band Wagon* and *Funny Face*. There

Astaire, Nanette Fabray, and Jack Buchanan in *The Band Wagon*

Astaire and Kay Thompson in *Funny Face*

were other heroes in these two: Audrey Hepburn, at her most entrancing, Jack Buchanan, Kay Thompson, Nanette Fabray, Cyd Charisse, Minnelli, Comden and Green, Gershwin, Schwartz and Dietz, Roger Edens, Stanley Donen, Richard Avedon, and the city of Paris. But primarily it was Astaire, blithe and bright. How sad then that both performed so unhappily at the box office that they were prime examples in the studios' decision that musicals were out.

Astaire in *The Band Wagon*

Danny Kaye and Vera-Ellen in *Wonder Man*

In this extraordinary period of original movie musicals, there were films other than those of Kelly and Astaire which should not be neglected. Danny Kaye is a superb buffoon and many of his movies gave him a chance to run the gamut of his many talents, although most of them were rickety vehicles with very little else to recommend them.

Danny Kaye in *Wonder Man*

Howard Keel and Jane Powell are not usually connected with the best ventures of the era. But one film in which they co-starred must be included with the very finest original movie musicals. This was *Seven Brides for Seven Brothers,* directed by Stanley Donen, and notable especially for some earthy humor and for some particularly lusty and virile dance numbers.

The Gallic waif, Leslie Caron, was the titular lead in *Lili* and *Gigi,* two unexpectedly highly successful screen musicals. *Lili* was a delicate thing, wistful and sentimental. Lerner and Loewe's *Gigi* was much more gaily sophisticated in the style of Colette from whose story it had come. *Lili* arrived at the point when everyone said musicals were dying; *Gigi* after they were long presumed dead. Oddly enough, when Miss Caron was to play *Fanny,* still another musical-show heroine, all of the Broadway songs were cut and served only as background music.

Leslie Caron in *Lili*

Louis Jourdan and Leslie Caron in *Gigi*

For movie musicals seemed through, killed, they said, by rising costs of production, apathy at the American box office, absolute antagonism in the continually more important foreign market. The success of *Gigi* seemed only the proverbial exception that proves the rule.

169

CHAPTER TEN

Broadway to Hollywood

ALMOST FROM the beginning, a principal source for the song-and-dance movies has been the hit show from the theatre. And about these transplanted Broadway shows, there is one statement that can almost invariably be made. The movie version is disappointing, at least in some degree, to those who saw the show. Favorite songs may be eliminated, favorite performers replaced. Try to find most of your pet Cole Porter songs in movie versions of *Mexican Hayride, Something for the Boys, Red, Hot, and Blue,* or *Let's Face It,* and only a couple of the most familiar were retained for *Anything Goes, Panama Hattie,* and *DuBarry Was a Lady.* Who has given the completely definitive performances in *Annie Get Your Gun* and *Gypsy?* Should anyone other than the great Merman even attempt to play either role in a screen version? Somebody did. And then there's the case of Audrey vs. Julie.

Even when a Broadway musical is transferred to the screen with all the loving care possible — that same *My Fair Lady,* for example — there is the vague feeling that it's just a record, a well-photographed play. Some of the urgency, the elation that is with an audience from the time the curtain goes up in the theatre is missing in the transfer to celluloid. The immense vitality of Robert Preston's personality in *The Music Man* leaps over the footlights. It's still there on screen, but much of the personal impact is gone.

Then, too, there is over-familiarity. By the time a Broadway

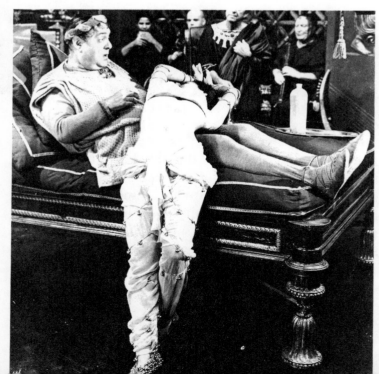

Zero Mostel and friend in *A Funny Thing Happened on the Way to the Forum*

musical hits your movie house, it has played for months, maybe for years. The thrill that comes with the discovery of a new musical comedy form in *Oklahoma!* for instance, can't be recaptured years later on film. Gwen Verdon can stop the show on Broadway with "Whatever Lola Wants" or Preston can with "Trouble," or Bolger's "Once in Love With Amy" and Alice Ghostly's "Boston Beguine" can have a theatre audience in a frenzy of excitement. But there are no show stoppers in the movies, even with the same personality doing the same numbers in their most technically perfect form. Spontaneity has disappeared.

Nor is casting always inspired. Gordon MacRae and Shirley Jones would have been perfectly acceptable leads in a second company of the stage *Carousel.* But you expect more than that from a major movie version of such a show. You need the extra voltage that could have been brought to it by performers of the caliber of, say, Frank Sinatra and Judy Garland. (To give them their due, they did try for Sinatra.)

There are exceptions — inspired moments when a sequence is adapted to the movie medium and the result is not only an effective way of filming the show but notably impressive as cinema. The opening shots of *West Side Story* are as breathtaking as anything ever put on the screen and, while sometimes the picture pales in contrast to the original, it is, particularly in the staging of its dance sequences, on the highest possible level for a movie musical. (Whether it's Jerome Robbins or Robert Wise, both billed, who deserves the major credit for all that was stunning about the film isn't really certain. Let's just divide it. But Wise is given complete credit for *Sound of Music,* far from the strongest of the Rodgers-Hammerstein musicals, but the most effectively filmed of them all.)

There are high hopes for *A Funny Thing Happened on the Way to the Forum,* previewed but not yet released at this writing. With Zero Mostel and Jack Gilford merrily re-creating their stage roles, assisted by zanies like Phil Silvers and Buster Keaton, it has been directed by Richard Lester. Lester's far-out directorial style (as demonstrated by *The Knack* and the Beatles' movies) has turned the highly successful Harold Prince Broadway production of the Burt Shevelove-Larry Gelbart-Stephen Sondheim show into an absolute madhouse of a movie. Almost everything works and the whole event is high hilarity. A special note for a special hero — Tony Walton for his production and costume design.

The original movie musical, prepared expressly for the screen, is still, when it is right, the most completely satisfying form of the entertainment, and most of the best movie musicals have been originals. But there are happy memories of many of those brought from stage to screen. On the following pages, a portfolio of some of them.

Lawrence Gray, Marilyn Miller, and others in *Sunny*

Anna Neagle and Ray Bolger in *Sunny*

One of the earliest musical movie stars was Marilyn Miller, who brought her Broadway successes, *Sally* and *Sunny,* to the screen. But neither Marilyn nor her movies made much of a movie dent and she went back to Broadway where her audience reaction would suit the title of her most brilliant show, *As Thousands Cheer.*

Some ten years or so later, *Sunny* was trotted out again — this time for the talents of Miss Anna Neagle. British audiences were fond of Miss Neagle, but she always seemed rather grawnd — the great lady slumming a bit — and, even with such talents as Ray Bolger in her casts, her musical films were throwbacks to the twenties.

The Marx Brothers were at their maddest when they did their stunts directly for films like *A Night at the Opera.* But their earliest period of moviemaking had them reprising shows, like *Animal Crackers,* which they had already tested on stage. And way back then, majestic Margaret Dumont was always very much in evidence.

Chico, Harpo, and Groucho Marx with Margaret Dumont in *Animal Crackers*

Fred Astaire, Ginger Rogers, and Irene Dunne in *Roberta*

Roberta was one Broadway confection that improved in transit to films. Most of the tuneful Jerome Kern score was retained, and the added numbers ("I Won't Dance," "Lovely to Look At") were Kern's, too, and quite up to standard. Add to that, the pretty soprano of pretty Irene Dunne and that new young dancey twosome, Fred Astaire and Ginger Rogers.

Kern's big classic *Show Boat* has been made three times — as a silent with a song prologue; as a mid-thirties success with Paul Robeson singing "Old Man River"; and as a splashy color special, with Kathryn Grayson as Magnolia and Ava Gardner as the vivid Julie.

Ava Gardner and Kathryn Grayson in *Show Boat*

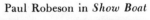
Paul Robeson in *Show Boat*

173

A pleasant, minor little Rodgers and Hart musical made a pleasant, minor little movie. It was *Too Many Girls* and the new, or semi-new, faces included Hal LeRoy, Ann Miller, Desi Arnaz, Frances Langford, and Eddie Bracken, among others, with Van Johnson among the chorus boys in the background.

Another of those rare ones that weathered well the journey to Hollywood was *Cabin in the Sky*. Of course, it kept Ethel Waters and such good numbers as "Taking a Chance on Love." And it added Eddie Anderson (good), Butterfly McQueen (better), and Lena Horne (best), plus such a great extra song as Harold Arlen-Yip Harburg's "Happiness Is a Thing Called Joe." It was directed with great taste by Minnelli.

Ronald Reagan, George Murphy, and Alan Hale in *This Is the Army*

Irving Berlin's big wartime revue, *This is the Army*, retained most of its stage spots (including Berlin's own singing of "Oh, How I Hate to Get Up in the Morning"), but added something of a story for those two future California politicians, Ronald Reagan and George Murphy.

Irving Berlin in *This Is the Army*

Good News was hardly that by 1947. But to the familiar old DeSylva, Brown, and Henderson songs was added a Betty Comden-Adolph Green-Roger Edens novelty, "The French Lesson," which has become something of a minor classic in its own right. Peter Lawford and June Allyson performed it.

Every so often, Hollywood uses a Broadway revue as basis for a movie musical. They sometimes add a story line and destroy what was notable on Broadway, such as the freshness of *Meet the People* (movie-ized with such familiars as Bert Lahr and Lucille Ball) or the outrageous gags of *Hellzapoppin'* (Martha Raye joined Olson and Johnson

Olsen and Johnson with Martha Raye in *Hellzapoppin'*

Bert Lahr and Lucille Ball in *Meet the People*

Fanny Brice and Hume Cronyn in *Ziegfeld Follies*

in the film). Or they may present it as straight revue, like *Ziegfeld Follies*, which mixed in newly created numbers with old stand-bys like "The Sweepstakes Ticket" — still fun with Fanny Brice and Hume Cronyn. *New Faces*, on the other hand, was a straight transcription from the stage with the lack of movie production values spoiling even such a standout as Alice Ghostly's "Boston Beguine."

Alice Ghostley in *New Faces*

177

Opera seldom comes to the movies, but it seldom comes to Broadway either. One that had its admirers in both media was Menotti's *The Medium*, with Marie Powers and Leo Coleman repeating their stage roles on film.

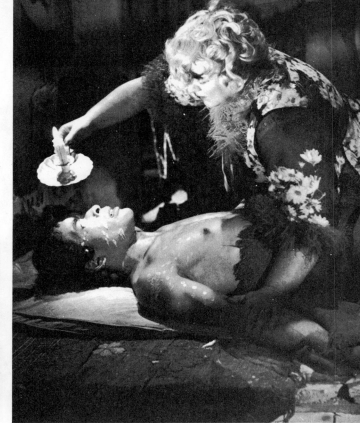

And Broadway's *Carmen Jones* was a dazzling innovation. Otto Preminger directed the movie version with a little less flair than its theatre staging, but it was still quite an experience. Harry Belafonte and Dorothy Dandridge were the ill-fated lovers.

Frank Sinatra was a good idea as *Pal Joey,* if you could forget the original Gene Kelly and his dances. But some of the best songs were cut and the sleazy clubs of the original were prettied up for Movieland. Add thoroughly conventional Hollywood casting in Rita Hayworth and Kim Novak as the girls in Joey's life.

Howard Keel's strong voice and personality only further exposed the creakiness of the old chestnut called *Kismet*.

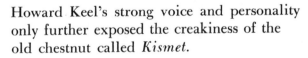

Ethel Merman, who usually loses out on re-creating her stage hits on screen, did manage to make it with *Call Me Madam*. Donald O'Connor was a big help, but it wasn't one of Merman's all-out triumphs in the theatre to begin with and movies didn't make much of it.

The Pajama Game was a well-made movie that kept most of what was fun in the stage version, including such bright people from the stage cast as John Raitt and dancing Carol Haney. Doris Day was a perfectly reasonable replacement for the original leading lady. With all of this, you would have expected a big, fat, movie hit, but it never quite reached that peak.

Damn Yankees was another made with a good bit of fidelity to the original. We still had Gwen Verdon as the seductive Lola, and Tab Hunter was quite all right as the compulsory "name" for the movie marquees. But it was just mild amusement in comparison to the stage show.

They had the right idea in *Guys and Dolls,* too. But Brando didn't try very hard as Sky Masterson and Sinatra was badly miscast as Nathan Detroit. Repeating her stage role, Vivian Blaine was still good. The only completely satisfying movie performance was by Jean Simmons, who brought more to her role than was there.

Julie Andrews in *The Sound of Music*

Surprisingly enough, the best movie version of any Rodgers and Hammerstein stage musical is the one most people felt was weakest on stage. This was *Sound of Music*, which looked like a real movie and not just a photographed stage play. And it had Julie Andrews who kept what could have been one of the gooiest roles of all time from getting too sticky. Another particularly

Julie Andrews and children in *The Sound of Music*

Deborah Kerr and Yul Brynner in *The King and I*

"The Small House of Uncle Thomas" ballet from *The King and I*

Gordon MacRae in *Oklahoma*

agreeable version was *The King and I*, with Deborah Kerr and Yul Brynner very right all the way in the leads, although the movie did have the feeling of photographed play about it. But "The March of the Siamese Children," the ballet, "Small House of Uncle Thomas," and most of the rest were as effective as in the theatre. The others, though — the lovely *Carousel*, the trailblazing *Oklahoma!* as well as *South Pacific* and one

"June Is Bustin' Out All Over" number from *Carousel*

France Nuyen, Juanita Hall, and John Kerr in *South Pacific*

that does not belong in the same league with these, *Flower Drum Song* — suffered in varying degrees from such handicaps as over-familiarity by the time the movie was released; surprisingly routine direction in a couple of cases; uninspired casting in many of the better roles. Even with their lapses, though, they were important pictures. They just couldn't quite live up to too-enthusiastic advance anticipation.

Nancy Kwan in *The Flower Drum Song*

It's hard to conceive of a bad performance of *Porgy and Bess* and although the movie version wasn't that, it was far from the experience for which we all had hoped. All the great songs were there and well sung. Sammy Davis was an electric Sporting Life, but such vibrant actors as Sidney Poitier and Dorothy Dandridge seemed curiously muted. And, although as a classic it should have been immune, it was so "cleaned up" that you almost expected the citizens of Catfish Row to begin speaking Oxford English.

If you liked *The Unsinkable Molly Brown* on Broadway — a negative vote from this corner — you must have like it quite as well on the screen. Debbie Reynolds worked hard and the picture did make money, lots of money. So they must have done something right.

Richard Beymer and Natalie Wood in *West Side Story*

George Chakiris and dancers in *West Side Story*

There were things wrong with the movie version of *West Side Story*, but why carp? The Leonard Bernstein-Stephen Sondheim-Arthur Laurents-Jerome Robbins triumph was brought to the screen with vast imagina-tion. It has been an enormous success, and one of the things most responsible, all over the world, for bringing back the fallen movie musical.

Chakiris, Beymer, and Russ Tamblyn in *West Side Story*

Judy Holliday, with Dean Martin as an added starter, brought her *Bells Are Ringing* hit to the movies. Vincente Minnelli directed, while the Comden-Green book and the Comden-Green-Jule Styne score remained as fresh. It was all very pleasant.

Janet Leigh danced energetically in the Shriners' number, and most of the rest of the things that had them cheering for Broadway's *Bye, Bye Birdie* were in the movie version. But not much of it worked very well on celluloid.

Robert Preston's superb vigor may have been
slightly confined by the movie screen, but he
was still the one and only "Music Man."
Like most of the better movie musicals, it
didn't quite recapture the magic of its best
stage performances. But it was plenty good
enough. The first movie musical, inciden-
tally, to sell for a million-dollar figure
to television.

By the time *My Fair Lady* made the movies, it was such An Event that going to see it was almost like going to church. George Cukor directed it reverently with scarcely a deviation from what was already tried and proven.

That included Rex Harrison, of course, and certainly nobody else would have dared try Professor Henry Higgins on screen. (The story goes that Cary Grant, invited to perform the role, announced, "Not only will I not

Wilfrid Hyde-White, Hepburn, and Harrison in *My Fair Lady*

play it, but if Rex Harrison doesn't do it, I won't even go to see it." Of course, the same story is told of Mr. Grant when he was asked to play the Robert Preston role in the movie, *The Music Man*.) Audrey Hepburn couldn't have been lovelier as the transformed Eliza Doolittle, but she couldn't erase memories of our elegant, aristocratic Audrey sufficiently

to be believable as the guttersnipe. Done lavishly, in high style, with all of its great stage moments lovingly preserved, and a big, big box office success to boot, what more could one have asked? We don't know, but we think there is something. Like excitement, perhaps.

Gladys Cooper, Jeremy Brett, Audrey Hepburn, Rex Harrison, and others in *My Fair Lady*

189

CHAPTER ELEVEN

Sing Me a Biography

How DO YOU write a song? Easy. You sit at a piano, think of Alexis Smith, listen to a faucet drip and a clock tick. Before long, you have composed the verse to "Night and Day." Cole Porter may not have found it that easy — but Cary Grant did in the movie about Porter's life.

Musical biographical movies are usually so unbiographical that they become jokes. Something vaguely resembling the life of the star or composer or musician is presented — all tidied-up and really just an excuse for introducing songs connected with their careers. The songs are usually pleasant to hear, the movies are frequently bores.

But you can't make a blanket statement. Because you keep remembering the good films about George M. Cohan and Al Jolson, Ruth Etting and Florenz Ziegfeld, Glenn Miller, and some of the others.

And you remember that *all* the movies about famous composers and stars and such were not quite the best pictures in your memory, but most of them had moments — scenes of songs and dances — that give them a good place in the history of musical movies.

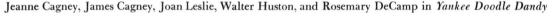

Jeanne Cagney, James Cagney, Joan Leslie, Walter Huston, and Rosemary DeCamp in *Yankee Doodle Dandy*

Cagney and chorus in *Yankee Doodle Dandy*

One way in which a regular anthology of popular songs can be brought to the screen is in the "musical biography." These range all the way from "— and then I wrote" mishmashes such as the Cole Porter or George Gershwin "stories" (have Alexis Smith as inspiration and you'll compose "Night and Day" or "Rhapsody in Blue") to something with as much imagination, excitement, and all-around entertainment value as *Yankee Doodle Dandy*, the story of George M. Cohan, his songs and career. Of course, this had an absolutely irresistible Jimmy Cagney spitting out the songs and strutting the dances, but here you could also accept the story line on which all those great musical numbers were strung.

191

Larry Parks in *The Jolson Story*

It was Al Jolson's own voice you heard in *The Jolson Story* and *Jolson Sings Again,* and Al practically seemed to take possession of the body of Larry Parks for one of the most accurate and enjoyable reincarnations to have shown up on film.

Larry Parks and Al Jolson

192

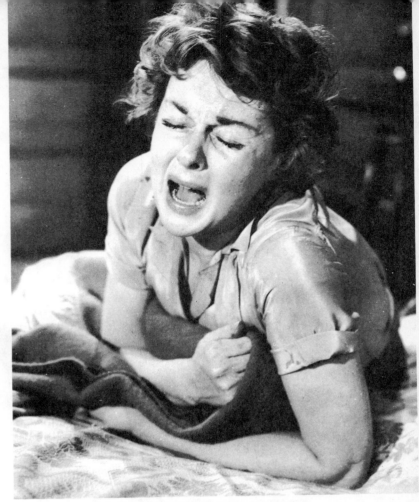

Susan Hayward in *I'll Cry Tomorrow*

Susan Hayward has re-created convincingly a couple of singing ladies, Jane Froman in *With a Song in My Heart* and Lillian Roth in *I'll Cry Tomorrow*. In both of these, the dramatic story line was stronger than usual, which made them even better as movie musicals.

Susan Hayword in *With a Song in My Heart*

193

The Ruth Etting story made hard-hitting material for Doris Day, with Cagney, in *Love Me or Leave Me.* Sorry the same can't be said for movies based on the lives of Helen Morgan, Texas Guinan, Eva Tanguay, Nora Bayes, Marilyn Miller, and Lillian Russell.

Pictures about our current-day composers usually don't turn out as well. One example, *Words and Music* with Tom Drake colorless as Richard Rodgers (even with such a lovely Dorothy as Janet Leigh) and Mickey Rooney completely overboard as Lorenz Hart.

Mickey Rooney, Eileen Janssen, Janet Leigh, June Hedin, and Tom Drake in *Words and Music*

Probably the granddaddy of all the movie musical biographies was that of the great showman himself. Because it was *The Great Ziegfeld*, there was an excuse for some of the most lavish musical-comedy production numbers. It was a film in which the characters themselves didn't suffer when the music turned off — not with William Powell as Ziegfeld, Myrna Loy as Billie Burke, Luise Rainer as Anna Held. And, happy day, Fanny Brice as herself.

Esther Muir, William Powell, and Fanny Brice in *The Great Ziegfeld*

But such films give a lot of "guest stars" a chance to shine in special numbers. *Words and Music,* for instance, had Gene Kelly's devastating "Slaughter on Tenth Avenue" ballet, danced with Vera-Ellen.·

It also had such an amusing interpolated number as the Judy Garland-Mickey Rooney "I Wish I Were in Love Again."

And the absolutely impossible "life story" of Jerome Kern had lots of stars doing Kern numbers right up to the spectacular finale with Frank Sinatra (on lower pedestal) leading a prominent group in the song after which the picture was titled, "Till the Clouds Roll By."

They're not all bad. *I'll See You in My Dreams* with Danny Thomas, as Gus Kahn, and Doris Day, his wife (and Patrice Wymore as that staple, the temperamental star), managed to be both touching and entertaining.

And *Three Little Words* (in which Arlene Dahl sang "I Love You So Much" and Debbie Reynolds became Helen Kane with help from Helen herself) had good moments in its story about Bert Kalmar and Harry Ruby.

Debbie Reynolds and Helen Kane

Mary Martin and Allan Jones sang the numbers in *The Great Victor Herbert* (Walter Connolly was "The Great" himself), but the picture was just one long hokey stage wait between songs.

Cole Porter wrote some never-to-be-forgotten songs, so some never-to-be-forgotten songs turned up in *Night and Day,* his movie "biography." This had Cary Grant as Porter, Porter's real-life friend Monty Woolley as Monty Woolley, and ladies like Alexis Smith (once again an "inspiration"), Jane Wyman (then still a cutie type), and Ginny Sims (like Jane Frazee, more familiar in the lower "B" stratum of musicals). In spite of them all, the movie was absolutely terrible.

Monty Woolley, Jane Wyman, and Cary Grant

It was pleasant to hear the Sigmund Romberg music in *Deep in My Heart,* but there was the usual lack of dramatic sustenance in the "biography" with José Ferrer playing "Rommy." Helen Traubel did everything but pratfalls to show she was even more of a "good Joe" than Lauritz Melchior, who usually played such roles.

Even with Robert Morley and Maurice Evans as the gentlemen of the title and the pot-pourri of their songs performed by the D'Oyly Carte company, *Gilbert and Sullivan* was just another in the parade of disappointing composer films.

Going back farther into history, *The Great Waltz* may not have been the definitive biography of Johann Strauss, but the Strauss music, as arranged by Tiomkin, and the lush presentation of the numbers, as directed by Julien Duvivier, made it look and sound like everything such a musical should be. Fernand Gravet was a rather gloomy fellow as Johann, a man saddled with a weepy wife (Luise Rainer) and another woman, played in old-time movie vamp style by Miliza Korjus.

On the whole, classic composers (Tchaikovsky, Liszt, Schumann, Rimski-Korsakov, etc.) have come off pretty badly in the movies based on their lives and music. One notable exception was *A Song to Remember* with Cornel Wilde as Chopin and Merle Oberon as George Sand. Nobody would hail it for its dramatic content or performances (Paul Muni was absolutely atrocious as the old music master), but the Chopin music was particularly well presented.

Stephen Bekassy, Cornel Wilde, and Merle Oberon in *A Song to Remember*

201

The Sol Hurok story (*Tonight We Sing*) was primarily an excuse for a compilation of numbers to appeal to the concert and opera devotees but it fulfilled its function well enough. The thin story presented David Wayne and Anne Bancroft as Mr. and Mrs. Hurok. Opera buffs also did well with *The Great Caruso* as sung by Mario Lanza (with Dorothy Kirsten and other leading opera stars), but nobody reaped any rewards from *So This Is Love*, in which Kathryn Grayson was Miss Grace Moore.

Best of the movie stories about the big-time bandleaders (other films covered Goodman, the Dorseys, Krupa, even John Philip Sousa) was *The Glenn Miller Story*. This benefited from Jimmy Stewart's typical, but pleasant, performance, with June Allyson, as usual, choking up but managing to smile bravely through her tears. Principal value, though, were all those nostalgic Glenn Miller numbers, well and generously presented.

CHAPTER TWELVE

Music in the Background

No, *The Trail of the Lonesome Pine* was not a musical and, as far as I know, none of these three stars ever sang a note. But "Melody From the Sky" and "Twilight on the Trail," as sung by Fuzzy Knight in the movie, were memorable songs. And because there were songs in the picture, it's an excuse to run this shot of my three favorite stars, bar none, (Sorry Greta, forgive me, Elizabeth!) Here then are Sylvia Sidney, Henry Fonda, and Beulah Bondi (with Fred Stone).

No song-and-dance girl she, but the films of Sylvia Sidney did produce some music to remember — the songs from *Trail of the Lonesome Pine,* or the lilting title tune from *Accent on Youth*. Some notable scores, too, all the way from Alfred Newman's *Dead End* with its feeling of the city to Kurt Weill's rather strange patter for *You and Me*. And, of course, *Street Scene* had the theme, by Newman, that would for two decades introduce most of the movies about Manhattan.

Elizabeth Taylor is another non-singer, but that didn't stop a record company from putting out an album of music from her movies. Here you could find Miklos Rozsa's theme music from *The V.I.P.'s*, part of the Alex North *Cleopatra* score, and others.

But the album missed the love theme by Franz Waxman which hauntingly underscored some of the most tender love scenes ever filmed, Taylor and Montgomery Clift in *A Place in the Sun*.

FROM THE Tiomkins and Korngolds to the present-day Mancinis, Previns, and Bacharachs, scores for dramatic films have become very much more than "Hearts and Flowers" played on a violin in the background of a sob scene. Much movie music is distinguished in its own right, frequently living on as an individual work of distinction long after the picture it served is forgotten. On these pages are scenes from a few of the films whose musical scores have stayed longest with me.

Humphrey Bogart and Lauren Bacall in *To Have and Have Not*

Musical stars, these two? Hardly. When Bacall asked Bogart to just "pucker up your lips and whistle," the response was hardly melodious. Yet a high spot of their movie meeting was when she draped herself across Hoagy Carmichael's piano and sang "How Little We Know" with "that look" direct to Bogie. And certainly nobody forgets the moment in an earlier movie — *Casablanca* — when the tormented Bogart finally forces himself to say those words, "Play it, Sam!" And an old tune got new life, with "As Time Goes By" achieving some kind of immortality as the love song of its whole time.

Joseph Sauers (later Sawyer), Gaylord Pendleton, Victor McLaglen, and Leo McCade in *The Informer*

Among the earliest dramatic film scores which made their own impression are the stunning *King Kong* score and the score that underlined the mood of *The Informer*. Both were by Max Steiner. Other notable Steiner scores are those for *Gone With the Wind*, and *Four Daughters*.

Charles Chaplin and Virginia Cherrill in *City Lights*

Some of the most tuneful melodies have come from Chaplin pictures — *City Lights, Modern Times*, and *Limelight*. The composer? Who else but the Little Man himself.

Rachmaninoff didn't mean it to be a movie score but his Second Piano Concerto provided one of the best as Celia Johnson sat, lost in the music and in her memories of a *Brief Encounter*.

Celia Johnson and Cyril Raymond in *Brief Encounter*

Often a musical composition of some note comes out of a film for which it has been composed. Richard Addinsell's "Warsaw Concerto" is still something of a classic; the film for which it was composed, *Suicide Squadron,* is barely remembered. The same is true for such compositions as "Cornish Rhapsody" and "Swedish Rhapsody," also from films.

The arresting Miklos Rozsa scores of *Spellbound* and *Lost Weekend* were intensified by being played on a strange musical instrument, the theremin, which added an eeriness to Gregory Peck's madness and Ray Milland's alcoholic horrors.

Ray Milland in *The Lost Weekend*

Orson Welles in *The Third Man*

Another unusual instrument, the zither, was
used for Anton Karas' "Harry Lime Theme"
better known after the title of its movie,
Carol Reed's *The Third Man*.

Leonard Bernstein has composed only one
motion-picture score, but it was a notable
one, the music for Elia Kazan's powerful
On the Waterfront.

Marlon Brando and Eva Marie Saint in *On the Waterfront*

William Holden and Beulah Bondi in *Our Town*

Marlon Brando and Vivien Leigh in *A Streetcar Named Desire*

Aaron Copland's rare film scores (*Our Town, Of Mice and Men, The Red Pony, The Heiress*) are considered distinguished additions to the body of his work.

Tennessee Williams' *A Streetcar Named Desire* was one major play which may have even gained in transit to the screen. One reason: the Alex North score. North has done other impressive scores, for example, *The Misfits, Who's Afraid of Virginia Woolf?* and *Spartacus*.

Vivien Leigh in *A Streetcar Named Desire*

Frank Sinatra in *The Man With the Golden Arm*

As one who loathed most of *The Man With the Golden Arm,* I'll admit the record album of its Elmer Bernstein score is one of my most-played. Other Bernstein scores are *To Kill a Mockingbird, A Walk on the Wild Side, The Magnificent Seven.*

Kim Novak and William Holden in *Picnic*

One of those dramatic musical moments you don't forget: when William Holden and Kim Novak begin to dance to "Moonglow" and the George Duning *Picnic* love theme sneaks into the background and takes over.

In decided contrast to his best-known musical themes for big costume specials (*Midsummer Night's Dream, The Sea Hawk, Adventures of Robin Hood, Elizabeth and Essex*) was Erich Wolfgang Korngold's score for *King's Row*, a somber study of small-town life.

Betty Field and Robert Cummings in *Kings Row*

Jennifer Jones, Gladys Cooper, and Joseph Cotten in *Love Letters*

Victor Young's scores frequently have a melody that can be lifted and turned into a popular song. Of these, "Love Letters" is my favorite; others are "Stella by Starlight" and "Around the World." Young also did the great score for *For Whom the Bell Tolls*.

Another whose musical scores usually produce a melody which becomes popular on its own ("Days of Wine and Roses," "Charade," "Moon River," "Pink Panther Theme," "Dear Heart," among examples) is the prolific Henry Mancini.

Lee Remick and Jack Lemmon in *Days of Wine and Roses*

Richard Burton, Elizabeth Taylor, George Segal, and Sandy Denis

"Shadow of Your Smile" is the most immediately identifiable theme from Johnny Mandel's fine *Sandpiper* score. *I Want to Live* and *The Americanization of Emily* are other Mandel scores of note.

If Mandel's music was the only noteworthy thing about *The Sandpiper*, the Burtons leaped back with something quite different and exciting. They, director Mike Nichols, and every other element of Edward Albee's searing *Who's Afraid of Virginia Woolf?* were lauded to the skies by the critics, and box-office returns were unprecedented. Here again, the music by Alex North (as previously noted) contributed greatly.

Paul Newman in *Harper*

Burt Bacharach is a young American composer whose motion-picture scores (*What's New, Pussycat?* and *Promise Her Anything,* are examples) have put him in demand. Andre Previn (*Harper, Elmer Gantry, Inside Daisy Clover*) is another whose scores are beginning to count.

Leslie Caron, Michael Bradley, and Warren Beatty in *Promise Her Anything*

216

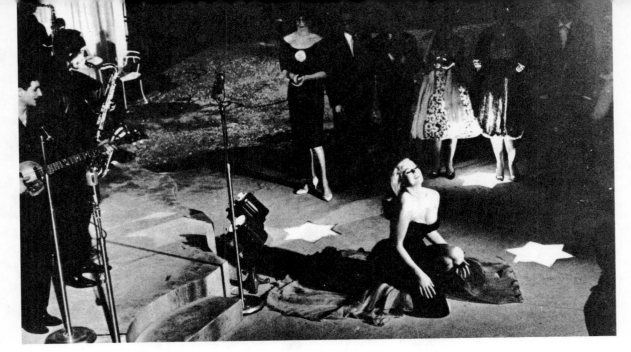

Anita Ekberg in *La Dolce Vita*

The whole *La Dolce Vita* mood was as quickly evoked by its Nino Rota score as by the Fellini film itself. Rota's scores for such Fellini films as *8½*, *La Strada*, and most of the others, are particular musical treats.

Many critics raved about Warren Beatty's Arthur Penn movie, *Mickey One*; others despised it. Much of the public was curiously apathetic. One thing that cannot be ignored is its Eddie Sauter score, as played by Stan Getz, already a jazz classic.

Warren Beatty in *Mickey One*

THESE, AS INDICATED, are only a few personal favorites in some thirty-five years of scored dramatic movies. There are notable omissions, it is realized. Richard Hageman, Bernard Herrmann, Dimitri Tiomkin, Herbert Stothart, Hugo Friedhofer, Werner Janssen, William Walton, Malcolm Arnold, Ernest Gold, Louis Gruenberg are others — and just a few of the others — who should have been represented. No word here about Hageman's *Long Voyage Home* score or Herrmann's *Citizen Kane* and *All That Money Can Buy*, about Newman's *How Green Was My Valley* and *Wuthering Heights*, Waxman's *Sunset Boulevard* and *Rebecca*, Tiomkin's *High Noon* and *Giant*, Maurice Jarre's *Lawrence of Arabia* and *Dr. Zhivago*, and many, so many more. But the point, it is hoped, has been made. Even in straight dramatic films, music is one of the major elements.

The Beatles

CHAPTER THIRTEEN

The Lean Years

BY THE MID-FIFTIES, the "Golden Era" of movie musicals indeed seemed over. Many of the brightest originals (*Funny Face,* for example, or *The Band Wagon* or *It's Always Fair Weather*) were making disappointing showings at the box office. As the world market became an ever more important factor in final box office grosses, it became evident that in many foreign countries musicals were not being shown at all. Or occasionally they would be shown with song numbers neatly snipped out. Some of the biggest song-star names (Howard Keel, Kathryn Grayson, Jane Powell, are examples) virtually disappeared from the screen. An aging, but certainly still nimble, Fred Astaire turned to non-dancing character roles, his true genius to be seen again only on an occasional television special. Gene Kelly, too, began to direct for the screen, theatre, and opera. Like Astaire, he has donned his dancing shoes only for some television shows. People like Doris Day and Leslie Caron now usually play non-musical roles.

For years, the Academy Awards for best songs have gone to pleasant, mostly unmemorable "pop" tunes spotted in non-musicals ("Three Coins in a Fountain," "Love Is a Many Splendored Thing," "Whatever Will Be," "Days of Wine and Roses," "Moon River," "Call Me Irresponsible") with only the Lerner-Loewe "Gigi" from a real movie musical breaking the cycle.

There were a few movie versions of Broadway musical comedies but, for the most part, these were pale reproductions of their sources.

"Original" movie musicals now became largely a matter of the dreary little program pictures that starred Elvis Presley, Pat Boone or, later, such "stars" as Frankie Avalon, Annette Funicello, and their "Beach Party" pictures.

This was the situation into the sixties. But there were new days to come, days beginning with the international success of *West Side Story*. And, ready to pump new life into a sick medium, were such widely varied starters as Julie Andrews and the Beatles.

He's practically a senior citizen now, but, my, what a fuss went up about Elvis Presley when he first burst into public consciousness on records, TV, and very shortly on the screen. Elvis wriggled and shouted, Elvis did bumps and grinds, Elvis wore sideburns and tight pants; in repose, he stared through hooded eyes and spoke through a sneering mouth. Elvis — unlike nice Pat Boone — was anything but the model for the clean-cut American boy. As a matter of fact, he became just that to a good percentage of young

America. The whole Elvis image was eventually to be modified and toned down but, by that time, the youngsters had even more far-out types for their hero worship, Sonny and Cher, for instance, and particularly Bob Dylan. The early Presley had a certain primitive excitement as a personality which didn't carry over to his movies. Almost without exception, they were cheap, routine programmers. But they made a lot of money and Elvis still manages to be a considerable draw.

Shirley Jones, Pat Boone in *April Love*

Pat Boone had a short vogue and he was more approved by adults than was Elvis, which is probably why he never made anywhere near the impact on the teen-agers. Most of his movies were deadly little bores. The most eventful thing that would happen in a Boone movie was his almost kissing Shirley Jones.

222

Ann-Margret in *Bye, Bye Birdie*

Nothing much turned up on the feminine side in the musicals of the lean years. Connie Francis and Annette Funicello were typical leading ladies in the few movie musicals there were. Ann-Margret was a good bet as she appeared opposite Elvis and did a few dances in a couple of other pictures like her teen-age spot in *Bye, Bye Birdie,* but soon she was sticking to straight, non-musical roles.

Ann-Margret and Elvis Presley in *Viva Las Vegas*

You might have thought of Natalie Wood as the major musical movie ingénue of the period. She was delightful in such generally satisfactory movie versions of top Broadway musicals as *West Side Story* and *Gypsy*. But her dancing wasn't really exceptional and her singing voice belonged to somebody else.

Pamela Tiffin in *State Fair*

Ann-Margret, Pat Boone in *State Fair*

Movie versions of Broadway hits continued to be made, although, even here, such shows as *Irma La Douce* and *Fanny* were filmed with their scores turned into background music. It was a bad time, though, for original movie musicals. There were only a few — the Cole Porter *High Society*, with Crosby, Sinatra, and Grace Kelly, was one; Lerner and Loewe's *Gigi* with Leslie Caron, another; and a remake of the original Rodgers-Hammerstein *State Fair* with some of the young hopefuls, Pamela Tiffin, Ann-Margret, Pat Boone, was another. Even though composed originally for films, it was now very old hat.

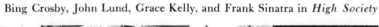

Bing Crosby, John Lund, Grace Kelly, and Frank Sinatra in *High Society*

225

Year after year, the Academy Award for the best movie song of the year went to a song written to be sung over the titles in a dramatic movie. Henry Mancini's "Moon River," for example, was crooned by Holly Golightly — and who knows whether Audrey herself or one of the Marni Nixon breed actually did the singing — but *Breakfast at Tiffany's* was hardly a musical.

There were signs that the movie musical might be coming back. Some of the screen versions of Broadway shows — particularly *West Side Story, My Fair Lady,* and *Sound of Music* — made enormous splashes at the box office, even in Europe which had previously disdained such shows. Their triumph is covered more thoroughly in Chapter Ten. And, for the first time in decades, a European-made musical movie caught some interest in the international market. This was *Umbrellas of Cherbourg* with its pretty Michel LeGrande music and its tired little soap-opera plot.

Nino Castelnuovo and Catherine Deneuve in *The Umbrellas of Cherbourg*

Paul McCartney and Wilfrid Brambell in *A Hard Day's Night*

But the big news from Britain were the Beatles' movies. The Beatles had already achieved a fantastic success as entertainment personalities, but who would have ever ex-

Paul McCartney, John Lennon, Ringo Starr, and George Harrison

Ringo Starr in *Help!*

The Beatles in *A Hard Day's Night*

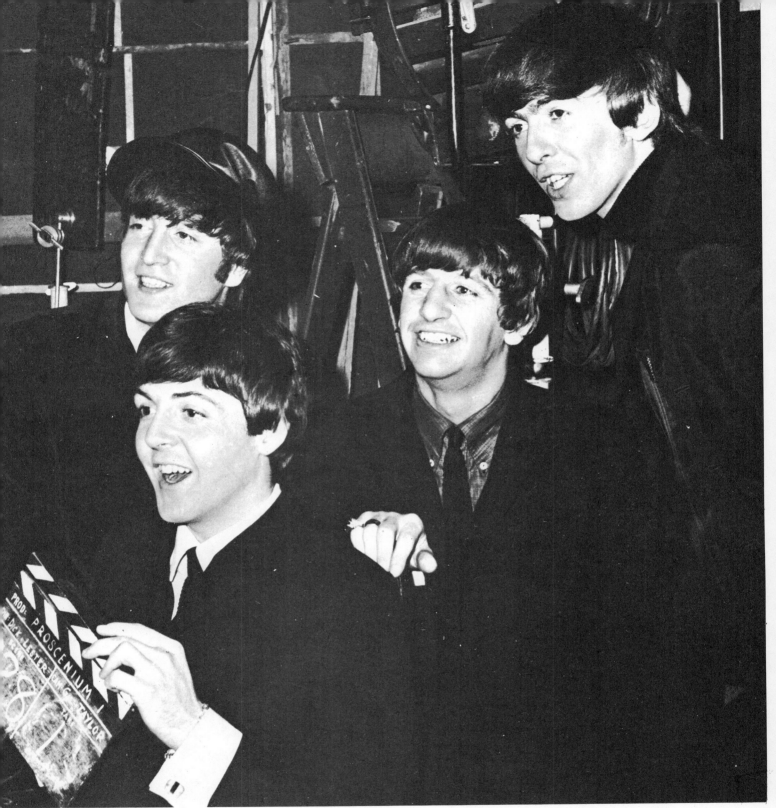

McCartney, Harrison, Starr, and Lennon

pected their pictures to be embraced by the critics as well. Both *A Hard Day's Night* and *Help!* with their zanily inventive direction by Richard Lester, were cheered. And the moptops turned out to be highly individual personalities in their own right.

Dick Van Dyke, Julie Andrews, Karen Dotrice, and Matthew Garber in *Mary Poppins*

And then there was Julie Andrews. Passed over for the role she had originated on Broadway in *My Fair Lady*, she retaliated by beating out her *Fair Lady* successor in awards. This was in Disney's *Mary Poppins*. It may not have been the *Mary Poppins* the purists wished to see (Beatrice Lillie was the only perfect casting for that and the story line sacrificed much of the sharp wit to rather sticky cuteness), but it filled theatres like

Van Dyke and Andrews in *Mary Poppins*

Van Dyke and Andrews in *Mary Poppins*

nothing of its type had done for years. And Julie Andrews, ably assisted by Dick Van Dyke, was a joy — crisp, cool, and lovely. And there was *The Sound of Music* to follow — and that was even more of a hit. Marshmallow it may have been, but Julie has a nice little caustic edge to her personality that keeps proceedings from getting too syrupy, Everyone is seeing it, and it looks like final proof that musicals are definitely back and big again.

Julie Andrews in *The Sound of Music*

CHAPTER FOURTEEN

Looking Ahead

WHAT'S TO COME in the musical world? At this writing, the Beatles are to do another one — a Western. Julie Andrews has been doing some straight non-musicals, but there had been hope that she would take to song again for the movie version of Lerner and Loewe's *Camelot*, in which she co-starred with Richard Burton on the stage. You just know that Warners wouldn't pass her over again for a repeat of another role she originated.

Vanessa Redgrave plays Anne Boleyn to Robert Shaw's Henry VIII in Fred Zinnemann's *A Man for All Seasons*

Richard Burton and Julie Andrews in *Camelot*

Betty Comden and Adolph Green

So they wooed Miss Julie, but a lot has happened since the days when she was ignored for *My Fair Lady* — she just wasn't available for *Camelot*. At this writing, Vanessa Redgrave, who scored in the hit *Morgan!*, has been named to play the part. The King Arthur, it seems likely as this is written, will be Richard Harris. Burton is too tied up with too many projects. He has agreed, though, with producer Arthur Jacobs and

Artist's conception of a scene from *Dr. Dolittle* with Rex Harrison

Allan Jones, Irene Hervey, and Jack Jones as a youngster

director Gower Champion to appear in an original movie musical by Terence Rattigan, with a score by Dory and André Previn. It's based on *Goodbye Mr. Chips,* and it's something special to anticipate.

There's happy news, too, in that many of the talents responsible for some of the best pictures of the "Golden Era" have been reunited for a new movie musical. Betty Comden and Adolph Green have written the

Irene Hervey and Jack Jones

Barbra Streisand

book . . . Arthur Freed will produce . . . Minnelli will direct. The picture: *Say It With Music*. The music is by Irving Berlin, and the whole prospect sounds promising — it makes you think of those gay days of *The Band Wagon* and *Singin' in the Rain*.

And one more particularly fascinating project — the all-time favorite "Dr. Dolittle" stories turned into a musical by writer-composer Leslie Bricusse, to be directed by the greatly versatile Richard Fleischer for Producer Arthur Jacobs. And the cast — Rex Harrison as the good doctor himself, with such stalwart supporters as Anthony Newley,

Lesley Ann Warren

Samantha Eggar, Hugh Griffith and all of those Dolittle animals.

Where will the new movie musical stars come from? They'll come from the theatre and TV, ballet and nightclubs, and there'll be some who'll make it without any previous background at all. Here are some predictions — just a few personal guesses. Any, or all, of them could be the next big stars of the musical movies.

There's Barbra Streisand — and it doesn't call for a crystal ball to venture that she'll have just as flamboyant a success in the movies as she has had on records, on tele-

Tommy Steele

Angela Lansbury

Lucine Amara

Phyllis Newman

Picture by Jerrold Schatzberg

vision and on Broadway. There are those who have even higher hopes for Phyllis Newman. The pert, bright-eyed comedienne is already a television favorite, and a few such appearances plus some theatrical work have conclusively demonstrated that she has even more appeal than the late, great Judy Holliday.

Jack Jones would be a best bet for movie

Picture by Timothy Galfas

Eddy Arnold

Victor Borge

musical stardom. He's already the hottest young star of the night club, television, and record worlds and he has the looks, personality, and great singing voice to carry him far in films. He has the heritage, too — his father is Allan Jones, his mother the charming Irene Hervey, who once graced a Gilbert and Sullivan movie most appealingly.

Perennial Angela Lansbury could conquer film musicals as she has won Broadway with *Mame*.

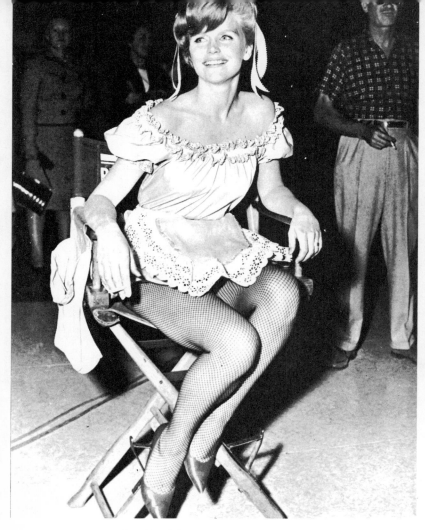

Lee Remick

Warren Beatty

Jordan Christopher, who became newsworthy as an Arthur "wild one," has proved versatile as a singing personality on his own. His first records are notable, and he has completed his first movie, *Return of the Seven*, as a dramatic star. Reports have him slated for movie stardom and, with his singing ability already well known, he might very well be a candidate for these lists.

Walt Disney is using Tommy Steele, Lesley Ann Warren, and John Davidson in his forthcoming *Happiest Millionaire*. They're fresh and talented personalities who have already proven themselves — Steele as a London teen-age idol and as the bright star of *Half a Sixpence* in the theatre ... Lesley Ann, who won personal critical raves in a Broadway disaster ... Davidson, who has shown up attractively on television.

Will there ever be another Grace Moore?

Maybe not — but, if movies do return to opera, there are opera stars as renowned for their beauty and acting ability as for their voices. Ladies like Lucine Amara, for example, or Anna Moffo.

Even now, Victor Borge is discussing the possibility of making his movie debut in a film in which, for the first time, he will play a character other than Borge. With his musical virtuosity and his deft comic style, he should have something new and noteworthy for the screen.

Gene Autry and Roy Rogers are not covered in this book, but to a large segment of the moviegoing public theirs were *the* movie musicals. There is a gentleman around now who may be considerably more polished than either of those two, but who sells records by the multi-millions to just such an audience. His name is Eddy Arnold.

240

Handsome, romantic, with a soaring voice, Sergio Franchi could take over the spot held so briefly by the late Mario Lanza.

And Hollywood itself may turn up some unexpected personalities who, already top stars in their own field, have the potentials for musicals, too. We'll say Warren Beatty — he has the flair and the versatility, and he can sing. And Lee Remick, who came out of a few-performance Broadway disaster and a much better television special to prove that she has all the elements that make a movie musical queen.

Gorgeous Jessica Walter has made her first big splash in movies this year. It's not generally known that she has a fine voice and turned down stage musicals in order to do dramatic films.

Jerome Robbins (with playwright Maria Irene Fornes)

Jessica Walter

Directors? Who, in the coming musical movie era, is apt to follow in the footsteps of the Minnellis, the Kellys, Donens, Berkeleys, and Lubitsch's? Jerome Robbins has already proved briefly — with minutes of *West Side Story* — that the screen can be as much his medium as theatre and ballet. Harold Prince, whose unfailing taste as a Broadway producer has carried through to his directorial assignments, may make his film debut as director of the screen version of one of his own Broadway shows. Joe Layton, heralded for his imaginative handling of the Barbra Streisand television specials, is another who should be able to bring new delights to the screen. And, of course, there is Mike Nichols, who has not yet directed a musical either on the stage or screen, (although, at this writing, he is about to go into rehearsals with one), but who has sufficiently demonstrated his genius so that the general impression is that he can do anything.

Sergio Franchi

Mike Nichols

Bert Stern is already known for his stunning documentary, *Jazz on a Summer Day,* which won distinction a few years ago. He has never followed up that first piece of movie-making, being too occupied as one of the top photographers for *Vogue* and *Life* — shooting still pictures of subjects like the dazzling ballet stars, Allegra Kent and Edward Villella. (And, if musicals with ballet flavor ever come back, what great movie stars these two could be!) Stern now has plans to return to film-making, as has another noted still photographer, Timothy Galfas. On the strength of Stern's already-demonstrated work with *Jazz* and Galfas' with some fascinating television projects — added to the brilliance of their still photography — it is safe to predict that they could be film-makers of originality, with the flair that spells excitement in movie musicals. Speaking of photographers and flair, don't forget the contribution of Richard Avedon to *Funny*

Ramsey Lewis

Face. If he decided to add movie-making to his activities, he would certainly join Stern and Galfas, as well as Nichols, Robbins, Prince, and Layton as the white hopes among new directors of movie musicals.

The Burt Bacharachs, Johnny Mandels, André Previns who have joined Mancini as imposing young talents composing scores and special songs for films may be joined

themselves by Ramsey Lewis. Lewis has become the darling of the "In" crowd as a musician. His talents go further, though, and he might very well become a composer of background scores.

Julie Andrews and the Beatles have led the way. Musical movies are with us again, stronger than they ever were. They could wane again — that has been the pattern — but they'll always, repeat *always*, come back.

Jordan Christopher

Edward Villella and Allegra Kent

Picture by Bert Stern

Appendix

A Personal Listing of Top Songs from the Musical Movies

FOLLOWING CHAPTERS ONE THROUGH FOUR are listings of particular favorites among the songs of the first musical movie era, as well as those associated with Bing Crosby, Fred Astaire, Dick Powell, and others involved in those chapters. No other personalities have such treasure troves of melody associated with their careers — although Judy Garland, Gene Kelly, and Alice Faye come close. This, then, is a listing of personal favorites from films not previously covered. The "personal" is an important adjective, for this listing does not begin to cover *all* of the songs. If there is a preponderance of songs from the thirties, blame it partially on the fact that those were the adolescent years for this chronicler. But there is also a firm belief that, for the most part, they're just not writing movie songs that way any more. I just can't find *one* original number from an Elvis Presley film, for example, that I would want to include on this list. And because "personal favorite" is the keynote, there is no hesitation in eliminating such numbers as "Mona Lisa" and "Three Coins in the Fountain," even if they did win Academy Awards. In all cases, the songs here were written directly for the screen. Music from other sources is not mentioned, no matter how impressive its screen performance may have been. Personalities who are particularly identified with the songs listed, or whose performances of them were especially memorable, are mentioned.

"Doing the Uptown Lowdown" (by Mack Gordon, Harry Revel) from *Broadway Through a Keyhole*.
"You Are Too Beautiful" (by Richard Rodgers, Lorenz Hart) from *Hallelujah, I'm a Bum*.
"Moon Song," "Twenty Million People" (by Sam Coslow, Arthur Johnston) sung by Kate Smith in *Hello Everybody*.
"They Call Me Sister Honky Tonk" (by Harvey Brooks, Gladys DuBois, Ben Ellison) sung by Mae West in *I'm No Angel*.
"You're My Thrill" (by Sidney Clare, Jay Gorney) from *Jimmy and Sally*.
"Isn't This a Night for Love?" (by Val Burton, Will Jason) from *Melody Cruise*.
"Ah, But Is It Love?," "Moonlight and Pretzels" (by E. Y. Harburg, Jay Gorney), "Are You Making Any Money?" (by Herman Hupfeld) from *Moonlight and Pretzels*.
"Gather Lip Rouge While You May" (by B. G. DeSylva, Leo Robin, Richard Whiting) from *My Weakness*.
"A Guy Who Takes His Time" (by Leo Robin, Ralph Rainger) sung by Mae West in *She Done Him Wrong*.
"Did You Ever See A Dream Walking?," "Good Morning, Glory," "Many Moons Ago" (Gordon, Revel) from *Sitting Pretty*.
"Give Me Liberty or Give Me Love" (Robin, Rainger) from *Torch Singer*.
"Love Songs of the Nile" (Arthur Freed, Nacio Herb Brown) from *The Barbarian*.
"Hold Your Man" (Freed, Brown) from *Hold Your Man*.
"I Cover the Waterfront" (Edward Heyman, Johnny Green) from *I Cover the Waterfront*.
"Johnny" (Edward Heyman, Frederick Hollander) sung by Marlene Dietrich in *Song of Songs*.
"Who's Afraid of the Big, Bad Wolf?" (Ann Ronell, Frank Churchill) from *Three Little Pigs*.
"This Little Piggie Went to Market" (Harold Lewis, Sam Coslow) from *Eight Girls in a Boat*.
"My Old Flame" (Coslow, Johnston) sung by Mae West in *Belle of the Nineties*.
"Waiting at the Gate for Katie" (Gus Kahn, Richard Whiting) from *Bottoms Up*.
"Stay As Sweet As You Are" sung by Lanny Ross, "Take a Number From One to Ten" sung by Lyda Roberti (Gordon, Revel) from *College Rhythm*.
"Keep On Doin' What You're Doin'" (Bert Kalmar, Harry Ruby) from *Hips, Hips Hooray*.

"I've Had My Moments" (Gus Kahn, Walter Donaldson) from *Hollywood Party*.

"Let's Fall in Love," "Love Is Love Anywhere" (Harold Arlen, Ted Koehler) from *Let's Fall in Love*.

"Ending With a Kiss" (Harlan Thompson, Lewis Gensler) sung by Lanny Ross in *Melody in Spring*.

"Boulevard of Broken Dreams" (Al Dubin, Harry Warren) from *Moulin Rouge*.

"Live and Love Tonight," "Cocktails for Two" (Johnny Burke, Sam Coslow, Arthur Johnston) sung by Carl Brisson, Kitty Carlisle in *Murder at the Vanities*.

"One Night of Love" (Gus Kahn, Victor Schertzinger) sung by Grace Moore in *One Night of Love*.

"With My Eyes Wide Open I'm Dreaming" (Gordon, Revel) sung by Dorothy Dell in *Shoot the Works*.

"Baby Take a Bow" sung by James Dunn, Shirley Temple, "This Is Our Last Night Together" (Lew Brown, Harry Akst) from *Stand Up and Cheer*.

"It Was Sweet of You," "Rock and Roll" (Sidney Clare, Richard Whiting), "If I Had a Million Dollars" (Johnny Mercer, Matty Melnick) from *Transatlantic Merry-Go-Round*.

"On the Good Ship Lollipop" (Clare, Whiting) sung by Shirley Temple in *Bright Eyes*.

"Sleepy Head," "Once in a Lifetime" (Gus Kahn, Walter Donaldson) from *Operator 13*.

"Riptide" (Kahn, Donaldson) from *Riptide*.

"All I Do Is Dream of You" (Brown, Freed) from *Sadie McKee*.

"A Little White Gardenia" (Sam Coslow) sung by Carl Brisson in *All the King's Horses*.

"Double Trouble" (Robin, Rainger, Whiting) sung by Lyda Roberti in *Big Broadcast of 1936*.

"You Are My Lucky Star," "I've Got a Feelin' You're Foolin'," "Broadway Rhythm" (Freed, Brown) — Frances Langford's singing, Eleanor Powell's dancing were most notable performances of these numbers in *Broadway Melody of 1936*.

"Animal Crackers in My Soup" (Ted Koehler, Irving Caesar, Ray Henderson) sung by Shirley Temple in *Curly Top*.

"Over My Shoulder," "When You've Got a Little Springtime in Your Heart" (Harry M. Woods) sung and danced by Jessie Matthews in *Evergreen*.

"Everything's in Rhythm With My Heart," "I Can Wiggle My Ears" (Maurice Sigler, Al Goodhart, Al Hoffman) sung and danced by Jessie Matthews in *First a Girl*.

"I'm in the Mood for Love," "I Feel a Song Coming On" (Dorothy Fields, Jimmy McHugh), sung by Frances Langford in *Every Night at 8*.

"I Was Lucky," "Rhythm of the Rain" (Jack Meskill, Jack Stern) sung by Maurice Chevalier in *Folies Bergere*.

"Now I'm a Lady" (Irving Kahal, Sam Coslow, Sammy Fain) sung by Mae West in *Goin' to Town*.

"I'm in Love All Over Again" (Fields, McHugh) from *Hooray for Love*.

"I Dream Too Much," "Jockey on the Carousel" (Fields, McHugh, Jerome Kern) sung by Lily Pons in *I Dream Too Much*.

"Lovely Lady," "I'm Shooting High" (Koehler, McHugh) from *King of Burlesque*.

"My Heart Is an Open Book," "Here Comes Cookie" (Gordon, Revel) from *Love in Bloom*.

"Alone" (Freed, Brown), "Cosi Cosa" (Ned Washington, Bronislaw Kaper, Walter Kurmann) sung by Allan Jones, Kitty Carlisle in *A Night at the Opera*.

"Paris in the Spring" (Gordon, Revel) sung by Mary Ellis in *Paris in the Spring*.

"Everything's Been Done Before" (Harold Adamson, Ed H. Knopf, Jack King) from *Reckless*.

"Accent on Youth" (Tot Seymour, Vee Lawnhurst) from *Accent on Youth*.

"In the Middle of a Kiss" (Sam Coslow) from *College Scandal*.

"Love Me Forever" (Kahn, Schertzinger) sung by Grace Moore in *Love Me Forever*.

"You Came to My Rescue," "Here's Love in Your Eye" (Robin, Rainger) from *Big Broadcast of 1937*.

"I've Got You Under My Skin," "Easy to Love," "Hey, Babe, Hey" (Cole Porter) from *Born to Dance*. (Although James Stewart, Virginia Bruce, and others participated, most notable performances were singing of Frances Langford, dancing of Eleanor Powell.)

"I'll Sing You a Thousand Love Songs" (Dubin, Warren) from *Cain and Mabel*.

"The Right Somebody to Love" (Jack Yellen, Lew Pollack) from *Captain January*.

"I Feel Like a Feather in the Breeze," "You Hit the Spot" (Gordon, Revel) sung by Frances Langford in *Collegiate*.

"It's Been so Long," "You," "You Never Looked so Beautiful" (Harold Adamson, Walter Donaldson) from *The Great Ziegfeld*.

"Head Over Heels in Love," "May I Have the Next Romance With You?" (Gordon, Revel) sung by Jessie Matthews in *Head Over Heels*.

"I Nearly Let Love Go Slipping Through My Fingers" (Harry M. Woods), "It's Love Again," "I've Got to Dance My Way to Heaven" (Sam Coslow) sung, danced by Jessie Matthews in *It's Love Again*.

"One in a Million," "Who's Afraid of Love?" (Sidney Mitchell, Lew Pollack) sung by Leah Ray in *One in a Million*.

"I Don't Want to Make History" (Robin, Rainger) sung by Frances Langford in *Palm Springs*.

"It's Love I'm After," "Balboa" (Mitchell, Pollack), the latter sung by Judy Garland in *Pigskin Parade*.

"When I'm With You," "But Definitely" (Gordon, Revel) sung by Alice Faye, Shirley Temple in *Poor Little Rich Girl*.

"Rendezvous With a Dream" (Robin, Rainger) from *Poppy*.

"If I Should Lose You" (Robin, Rainger) sung by Gladys Swarthout in *Rose of the Rancho*.

"I Have the Room Above," "Gallivantin' Around," "Ah Still Suits Me" (Oscar Hammerstein II, Jerome Kern) from *Show Boat*.

"When Did You Leave Heaven?" (Walter Bullock, Richard Whiting), "Sing, Baby, Sing" (Yellen, Pollack), "You Turned the Tables on Me" (Sidney Mitchell, Louis Alter) sung by Alice Faye, Tony Martin in *Sing, Baby, Sing*.

"Goodnight My Love" (Gordon, Revel) sung by Alice Faye in *Stowaway*.

"I'm in a Dancing Mood" (Sigler, Goodhart, Hoffman) sung by Jack Buchanan in *This'll Make You Whistle*.

"Smoke Dreams" (Freed, Brown) from *After the Thin Man*.

"When You're Dancing the Waltz" (Richard Rodgers, Lorenz Hart) from *Dancing Pirate*.

"Awake in a Dream" (Leo Robin, Frederick Hollander) sung by Marlene Dietrich in *Desire*.

"The World Is Mine Tonight" (Holt Marvell, George Posford) sung by Nino Martini in *The Gay Desperado*.

"With All My Heart" (Gus Kahn, Jimmy McHugh) from *Her Master's Voice*.

"Moonlight and Shadows" (Robin, Hollander) sung by Dorothy Lamour in *Jungle Princess*.

"San Francisco" (Gus Kahn, Bronislaw Kaper), "Would You?" (Brown, Freed) sung by Jeanette MacDonald in *San Francisco*.

"Did I Remember?" (Adamson, Donaldson) from *Suzy*.

"Melody From the Sky," "Twilight on the Trail" (Paul Francis Webster, Louis Alter) from *Trail of the Lonesome Pine*.

"Swing Is Here to Sway" (Gordon, Revel) from *Ali Baba Goes to Town*.

"Whispers in the Dark" (Robin, Hollander) sung by Connee Boswell in *Artists and Models*.

"Blossoms on Broadway" (Robin, Rainger) from *Blossoms on Broadway*.

"Champagne Waltz" (Milton Drake, Ben Oakland, Con Conrad) sung by Gladys Swarthout in *Champagne Waltz*.

"All God's Chillun Got Rhythm" (Kahn, Jurmann, Kaper) from *A Day at the Races*.

"Donkey Serenade" (Bob Wright, Chet Forrest, Rudolph Friml) sung by Allan Jones in *Firefly*.

"Gangway" (Sol Lerner, Al Hoffman, Al Goodhart) from *Gangway*.

"Can I Forget You?" "Folks Who Live on the Hill"

(Oscar Hammerstein II, Jerome Kern) sung by Irene Dunne in *High, Wide and Handsome*.

"Was It Rain?" (Lou Handman, Walter Hirsch) sung by Frances Langford in *Hit Parade*.

"I Hit a New High" (Harold Adamson, Jimmy McHugh) from *Hitting a New High*.

"I'll Take Romance" (Oscar Hammerstein II, Ben Oakland) sung by Grace Moore in *I'll Take Romance*.

"Life of the Party" (Herb Magidson, Allie Wrubel), "Roses in December" (Magidson, George Jessel, Ben Oakland) from *Life of the Party*.

"You're My Dish" (Adamson, McHugh) from *Merry-Go-Round of 1938*.

"Our Penthouse on Third Avenue" (Lew Brown, Sammy Fain) from *New Faces of 1937*.

"In the Still of the Night," "Rosalie" (Cole Porter) sung by Nelson Eddy, danced by Eleanor Powell, in *Rosalie*.

"Swing High, Swing Low" (Ralph Freed, Burton Lane) from *Swing High, Swing Low*.

"Is It Love or Infatuation?" (Coslow, Hollander) from *This Way Please*.

"Blame It on the Rhumba," "Where Are You?" (Adamson, McHugh) sung by Gertrude Niesen in *Top of the Town*.

"Turn Off the Moon" (Sam Coslow) from *Turn Off the Moon*.

"Never in a Million Years," "There's a Lull in My Life," "It's Swell of You," "Wake Up and Live" (Gordon, Revel) sung by Buddy Clark (for Jack Haley) and Alice Faye in *Wake Up and Live*.

"That Old Feeling" (Lew Brown, Sammy Fain) from *Vogues of 1938*.

"You Can't Have Everything," "The Loveliness of You," "Afraid to Dream" (Gordon, Revel) sung by Alice Faye in *You Can't Have Everything*.

"You're a Sweetheart" (Adamson, McHugh) sung by Alice Faye in *You're a Sweetheart*.

"Danger, Love at Work" (Gordon, Revel) from *Danger, Love at Work*.

"Easy Living" (Robin, Rainger) from *Easy Living*.

"Moon of Manakoora" (Frank Loesser, Alfred Newman) from *The Hurricane*.

"Always and Always" (Chet Forrest, Bob Wright, Edward Ward) from *Mannequin*.

"Someone to Care for Me" (Kahn, Kaper, Jurmann) sung by Deanna Durbin in *Three Smart Girls*.

"True Confession" (Coslow, Hollander) from *True Confession*.

"Our Song" (Dorothy Fields, Jerome Kern) sung by Grace Moore in *When You're in Love*.

"A Thousand Dreams of You" (Webster, Alter) from *You Only Live Once*.

"Heigh Ho," "Whistle While You Work," "One Song," "With a Smile and a Song," "Some Day My

Prince Will Come," "Silly Song," "I'm Wishing" (Larry Morey, Frank Churchill) from *Snow White and the Seven Dwarfs*.

"Now It Can Be Told" (sung by Alice Faye), "My Walking Stick" (sung by Ethel Merman), both by Irving Berlin from *Alexander's Ragtime Band*.

"Thanks for the Memory" (Robin, Rainger) sung by Bob Hope, Shirley Ross in *The Big Broadcast of 1938*.

"Says My Heart" (Frank Loesser, Burton Lane), "You Leave Me Breathless" (Ralph Freed, Frederick Hollander) sung by Harriet Hilliard, Fred MacMurray in *Cocoanut Grove*.

"Moments Like This," "How'dja Like to Love Me?" (Loesser, Lane) from *College Swing*.

"What Goes on Here in My Heart?" (Robin, Rainger) from *Give Me a Sailor*.

"Love Walked In," "Love Is Here to Stay," "I Was Doing All Right" (Ira and George Gershwin), "Spring Again" (Ira Gershwin, Kurt Weill) sung by Kenny Baker, Ella Logan in *Goldwyn Follies*.

"Where in the World" (Gordon, Revel) from *Josette*.

"You Couldn't be Cuter" (Dorothy Fields, Jerome Kern) from *Joy of Living*.

"Meet the Beat of My Heart" (Gordon, Revel), "In Between" (Roger Edens) sung by Judy Garland in *Love Finds Andy Hardy*.

"Serenade to the Stars," "I Love to Whistle" (Adamson, McHugh) sung by Deanna Durbin in *Mad About Music*.

"I've Got a Date With a Dream" (Gordon, Revel) from *My Lucky Star*.

"Good Night, Angel," "Speak Your Heart," "Swingin' in the Corn" (Herb Magidson, Allie Wrubel) from *Radio City Revels*.

"An Old Straw Hat" (Gordon, Revel) sung by Shirley Temple in *Rebecca of Sunnybrook Farm*.

"Daughter of Mademoiselle" (Sidney Clare, Harry Akst) from *Battle of Broadway*.

"Beside a Moonlight Stream" (Coslow, Hollander) from *Booloo*.

"How Can You Forget?" (Rodgers, Hart) from *Fools for Scandal*.

"Two Sleepy People" (Loesser, Carmichael) sung by Bob Hope, Shirley Ross in *Thanks for the Memory*.

"You and Me" (Freed, Hollander) from *You and Me*.

"You're Only Young Once" (Chet Forrest, Bob Wright, Alexander Hyde) from *You're Only Young Once*.

"God's Country" (E. Y. Harburg, Harold Arlen), "Good Morning" (Freed, Brown), sung by Douglas McPhail, Judy Garland, Mickey Rooney in *Babes in Arms*.

"At the Balalaika" (Wright, Forrest, Stothart) sung by Nelson Eddy in *Balalaika*.

"Lydia, the Tattooed Lady" (Harburg, Arlen) sung by Groucho Marx in *Day at the Circus*.

"Faithful Forever" (Robin, Rainger) from *Gulliver's Travels*.

"Strange Enchantment" (Loesser, Hollander) from *Man About Town*.

"I Never Knew Heaven Could Speak" (Gordon, Revel) sung by Alice Faye in *Rose of Washington Square*.

"I Go for That" (Loesser, Melnick) sung by Dorothy Lamour in *St. Louis Blues*.

"I Poured My Heart Into a Song," "I'm Sorry for Myself," "Back to Back" (Irving Berlin), sung by Mary Healy, Rudy Vallee, in *Second Fiddle*.

"Over the Rainbow," "If I Only Had a Heart," "Merry Old Land of Oz," "We're Off to See the Wizard," "Ding, Dong, the Witch Is Dead" (Harburg, Arlen) sung by Judy Garland, Bert Lahr, Ray Bolger, Jack Haley in *Wizard of Oz*.

"You've Got That Look," "See What the Boys in the Back Room Will Have" (Loesser, Hollander) sung by Marlene Dietrich in *Destry Rides Again*.

"How Strange" (Kahn, Stothart) from *Idiot's Delight*.

"Intermezzo" (Robert Henning, Heinz Provost) from *Intermezzo*.

"Wishing" (B. G. DeSylva), "Sing My Heart" (Ted Koehler, Harold Arlen) sung by Irene Dunne in *Love Affair*.

"I'm in Love With the Honorable Mr. So and So" (Sam Coslow) sung by Virginia Bruce in *Society Lawyer*.

"The Lady's in Love With You" (Loesser, Lane) sung by Shirley Ross, Bob Hope in *Some Like It Hot*.

"Say It" (Loesser, McHugh) from *Buck Benny Rides Again*.

"South American Way" (Al Dubin, Jimmy McHugh) sung by Carmen Miranda, "Down Argentine Way" (Gordon, Warren) from *Down Argentine Way*.

"Blue Lovebird" (Gus Kahn, Bronislaw Kaper) from *Lillian Russell*.

"It's a Great Day for the Irish," "Pretty Girl Milking Her Cow" (Roger Edens) sung by Judy Garland in *Little Nellie Kelly*.

"It's a Blue World" (Forrest, Wright) from *Music in My Heart*.

"Remind Me" (Dorothy Fields, Jerome Kern) from *One Night in the Tropics*.

"Our Love Affair" (Freed, Edens) sung by Judy Garland, Mickey Rooney in *Strike Up the Band*.

"Fifth Avenue" (Gordon, Revel) from *Young People*.

"You've Got Me This Way" (Johnny Mercer, Jimmy McHugh) from *You'll Find Out*.

"Angel in Disguise" (Kim Gannon, Stephen Weiss, Paul Mann) from *It All Came True*.

"I've Been in Love Before" (Loesser, Hollander) sung by Marlene Dietrich in *Seven Sinners*.

"Where Was I?" (Al Dubin, W. Franke Harling) from *'Til We Meet Again*.

"You Say the Sweetest Things, Baby" (Gordon, Revel) sung by Alice Faye, John Payne in *Tin Pan Alley*.

"When You Wish Upon a Star," "Got No Strings," "Hi-Diddle-Dee-Dee" (Ned Washington, Leigh Harline) from *Pinocchio*.

"How About You?" (Ralph Freed, Burton Lane) sung by Judy Garland, Mickey Rooney in *Babes on Broadway*.

"Tenement Symphony" (Sid Kuller, Ray Golden, Hal Borne) sung by Tony Martin in *The Big Store*.

"Blues in the Night," "This Time the Dream's on Me" (Mercer, Arlen) from *Blues in the Night*.

"I Hear Music" (Loesser, Lane) from *Dancing on a Dime*.

"I'll Never Let a Day Pass By," "Kiss the Boys Goodbye" (Schertzinger, Loesser) sung by Mary Martin in *Kiss the Boys Goodbye*.

"The Last Time I Saw Paris" (Oscar Hammerstein II, Jerome Kern), "Your Words and My Music" (Arthur Freed, Roger Edens) from *Lady Be Good*.

"Dolores" (Loesser, Lewis Alter) performed by Tommy Dorsey's Orchestra in *Las Vegas Nights*.

"Chattanooga Choo Choo," "I Know Why," "At Last" (Gordon, Warren) as performed by the Glenn Miller Orchestra in *Sun Valley Serenade*.

"Chica Chica Boom Chic," "I Yi Yi Yi Yi, I Like You Very Much" (Gordon, Warren) sung by Carmen Miranda in *That Night in Rio*.

"Minnie from Trinidad" (Roger Edens), "You Stepped Out of a Dream" (Gus Kahn, Nacio Herb Brown) from *Ziegfeld Girl*.

"We're the Couple in the Castle" (Loesser, Carmichael) from *Mr. Bug Goes to Town*.

"I Remember You," "The Fleet's In," "Arthur Murray Taught Me Dancing in a Hurry," "Not Mine" (Johnny Mercer, Victor Schertzinger), "Tangerine" (Frank Loesser, Schertzinger) performed by Dorothy Lamour, Betty Hutton, Jimmy Dorsey's Orchestra in *The Fleet's In*.

"There Will Never Be Another You" (Mack Gordon, Harry Warren) from *Iceland*.

"Kalamazoo," "Serenade in Blue" (Gordon, Warren) performed by Glenn Miller's Orchestra in *Orchestra Wives*.

"Can't Get Out of This Mood" (Frank Loesser, Jimmy McHugh) from *Seven Days Leave*.

"I Had the Craziest Dream," "I Like to Be Loved By You" (Gordon, Warren) latter sung by Carmen Miranda in *Springtime in the Rockies*.

"That Old Black Magic" (Mercer, Arlen) sung by Johnnie Johnston in *Star-Spangled Rhythm*.

"I Don't Want to Walk Without You," "I Said No" (Loesser, Jule Styne) from *Sweater Girl*.

"Jingle Jangle Jingle" (Joseph J. Lilley) from *Forest Rangers*.

"I've Heard That Song Before" (Sammy Cahn, Jule Styne) from *Youth on Parade*.

"Happiness is a Thing Called Joe" (Harburg, Arlen) sung by Ethel Waters in *Cabin in the Sky*.

"No Love, No Nothing" (Robin, Warren) sung by Alice Faye in *The Gang's All Here*.

"Murder He Says" (Loesser, McHugh) sung by Betty Hutton in *Happy Go Lucky*.

"You'll Never Know" (Gordon, Warren) sung by Alice Faye in *Hello, Frisco, Hello*.

"I Couldn't Sleep a Wink," "Lovely Way to Spend an Evening," "The Music Stopped" (Adamson, McHugh) sung by Frank Sinatra in *Higher and Higher*.

"You'd Be So Nice To Come Home To" (Cole Porter) from *Something to Shout About*.

"My Heart Tells Me" (Gordon, Warren) sung by Betty Grable in *Sweet Rosie O'Grady*.

"They're Either Too Young or Too Old" sung by Bette Davis, "How Sweet You Are," "The Dreamer" sung by Dinah Shore, "Thank Your Lucky Stars" (Loesser, Arthur Schwartz) from *Thank Your Lucky Stars*.

"The Joint Is Really Jumping" (Ralph Blane, Hugh Martin) from *Thousands Cheer*.

"It Could Happen to You," "The Rocking Horse Ran Away" (Johnny Burke, Jimmy Van Heusen) sung respectively by Dorothy Lamour, Betty Hutton in *And the Angels Sing*.

"Like Someone in Love," "Sleighride in July" (Burke, Van Heusen) sung by Dinah Shore in *Belle of the Yukon*.

"Milkman, Keep Those Bottles Quiet" (Don Raye, Gene DePaul) sung by Nancy Walker in *Broadway Rhythm*.

"More and More" (E. Y. Harburg, Jerome Kern) sung by Deanna Durbin in *Can't Help Singing*.

"Put Me to the Test," "Make Way for Tomorrow," "Long Ago and Far Away" (Ira Gershwin, Jerome Kern, E. Y. Harburg) performed by Rita Hayworth, Gene Kelly, Phil Silvers in *Cover Girl*.

"I'll Walk Alone" (Sammy Cahn, Jule Styne) from *Follow the Boys*.

"There's a Fellow Waiting in Poughkeepsie" (Mercer, Arlen) sung by Betty Hutton in *Here Come the Waves*.

"Don't Fence Me In" (Cole Porter) from *Hollywood Canteen*.

"Trolley Song," "The Boy Next Door," "Have Yourself a Merry Little Christmas," "Skip to My Lou" (Ralph Blanc, Hugh Martin) sung by Judy Garland in *Meet Me in St. Louis*.

"Come Out Wherever You Are" (Cahn, Styne) sung by Frank Sinatra in *Step Lively*.

"I'm Making Believe" (Mack Gordon, Jimmy Monaco) from *Sweet and Low Down*.

"Now I Know," "Tess' Torch Song" (Koehler, Arlen) sung by Dinah Shore in *Up in Arms*.

"Spring Will Be a Little Late" (Loesser) sung by Deanna Durbin in *Christmas Holiday*.

"Laura" (David Raksin, Johnny Mercer) from *Laura*.

"In My Arms" (Loesser, Ted Grouya) from *See Here, Private Hargrove*.

"How Little We Know" (Mercer, Carmichael) from *To Have and Have Not*.

"Three Caballeros" (Charles Wolcott), "You Belong to My Heart" (Roy Gilbert, Augustin Lara) from *Three Caballeros*.

"I Begged Her," "I Fall in Love Too Easily" (Cahn, Styne) sung by Gene Kelly, Frank Sinatra in *Anchors Aweigh*.

"The More I See You," "In Acapulco" (Gordon, Warren) from *Diamond Horseshoe*.

"Hubba, Hubba, Hubba," "Here Comes Heaven Again" (Adamson, McHugh) sung by Perry Como in *Doll Face*.

"I Can't Begin to Tell You" (Mack Gordon, Jimmy Monaco) from *The Dolly Sisters*.

"I'll Buy That Dream" (Magidson, Wrubel) from *Sing Your Way Home*.

"It Might as Well Be Spring," "My State Fair," "All I Owe I-O-Way," "That's for Me," "Isn't It Kind of Fun," "It's a Grand Night for Singing" (Oscar Hammerstein II, Richard Rodgers) sung by Dick Haymes, Vivian Blaine, others in *State Fair*.

"Doctor, Lawyer, Indian Chief" (Paul Francis Webster, Hoagy Carmichael), "Square in the Social Circle" (Ray Evans, Jay Livingston) sung by Betty Hutton in *Stork Club*.

"I Should Care" (Sammy Cahn, Alex Stordahl, Paul Weston) from *Thrill of a Romance*.

"Tonight and Every Night" (Cahn, Styne) from *Tonight and Every Night*.

"Love Letters" (Victor Young) from *Love Letters*.

"As Long as I Live" (Charles Tobias, Max Steiner) from *Saratoga Trunk*.

"Stella by Starlight" (Ned Washington, Victor Young) from *The Uninvited*.

"In Love in Vain," "All Through the Day," "Up With the Lark" (Leo Robin, Oscar Hammerstein II, Jerome Kern) from *Centennial Summer*.

"Do You Love Me?" (Harry Ruby) sung by Dick Haymes in *Do You Love Me?*.

"On the Atchison, Topeka and Santa Fe" (Mercer, Warren) sung by Judy Garland in *The Harvey Girls*.

"My Heart Goes Crazy" (Johnny Burke, Jimmy Van Heusen) from *London Town*.

"Zip-a-Dee-Doo-Dah" (Ray Gilbert, Allie Wrubel),

"Sooner or Later" (Gilbert, Charles Wolcott) from *Song of the South*.

"Somewhere in the Night," "On the Boardwalk in Atlantic City," "You Make Me Feel So Young" (Mack Gordon, Joseph Myrow) from *Three Little Girls in Blue*.

"A Gal in Calico," "Oh, But I Do," "Rainy Night in Rio" (Leo Robin, Arthur Schwartz) from *The Time, The Place and The Girl*.

"Love" (Ralph Blane, Hugh Martin) sung by Lena Horne in *Ziegfeld Follies*.

"Put the Blame on Mame" (Doris Fisher, Allan Roberts) performed by Rita Hayworth with a reported dubbed voice in *Gilda*.

"Mamselle" (Mack Gordon, Edmund Goulding) from *The Razor's Edge*.

"Can It Be Wrong" (Kim Gannon, Max Steiner) from *Now Voyager*.

"To Each His Own" (Ray Evans, Jay Livingston) from *To Each His Own*.

"Tomorrow is Forever" (Charles Tobias, Max Steiner) from *Tomorrow is Forever*.

"The French Lesson" (Betty Comden, Adolph Green, Roger Edens), "Pass That Peace Pipe" (Ralph Blane, Hugh Martin) from *Good News*.

"Time After Time" (Cahn, Styne) sung by Frank Sinatra in *It Happened in Brooklyn*.

"You Do," "Kokomo, Indiana" (Mack Gordon, Josef Myrow) performed by Betty Grable, Dan Dailey in *Mother Wore Tights*.

"Papa, Don't Preach to Me," "I Wish I Didn't Love You So" (Frank Loesser) sung by Betty Hutton in *Perils of Pauline*.

"Aren't You Kinda Glad We Did," "Changing My Tune," "For You, for Me, for Evermore" (Ira and George Gershwin) from *The Shocking Miss Pilgrim*.

"Tallahassee," "He Can Waltz" (Frank Loesser) from *Variety Girl*.

"Golden Earrings" (Ray Evans, Jay Livingston, Victor Young) from *Golden Earrings*.

"Ivy" (Hoagy Carmichael) from *Ivy*.

"You're Not so Easy to Forget" (Magidson, Oakland) from *Song of the Thin Man*.

"You May Not Remember" (George Jessel, Ben Oakland) sung by Anne Jeffreys in *Trail Street*.

"It Was Written in the Stars," "For Every Man There's a Woman," "Hooray for Love" (Leo Robin, Harold Arlen) sung by Tony Martin in *Casbah*.

"It's a Most Unusual Day" (Adamson, McHugh) sung by Jane Powell in *A Date With Judy*.

"Black Market," "Ruins of Berlin" (Frederick Hollander) sung by Marlene Dietrich in *A Foreign Affair*.

"Love Is Where You Find It" (Edward Heyman, Earl Brent, Nacio Herb Brown) sung by Kathryn Grayson in *The Kissing Bandit*.

"Love of My Life," "Mack the Black," "You Can Do No Wrong," "Be a Clown" (Cole Porter) performed by Gene Kelly, Judy Garland in *The Pirate*.

"It's Magic" (Cahn, Styne) sung by Doris Day in *Romance on the High Seas*.

"It's Our Home Town," "Afraid to Fall in Love," "Stanley Steamer" (Ralph Blane, Harry Warren) from *Summer Holiday*.

"This is the Moment" (Leo Robin, Frederick Hollander) from *That Lady in Ermine*.

"Buttons and Bows" (Ray Evans, Jay Livingston) sung by Bob Hope, Jane Russell in *Paleface*.

"Baby, It's Cold Outside" (Frank Loesser) from *Neptune's Daughter*.

"Farewell Amanda" (Cole Porter) from *Adam's Rib*.

"My Foolish Heart" (Washington, Young) from *My Foolish Heart*.

"So This Is Love," "Cinderella" (Mack David, Al Hoffman, Jerry Livingston) from *Cinderella*.

"Be My Love" (Sammy Cahn, Nicholas Brodszky) sung by Mario Lanza in *Toast of New Orleans*.

"The Laziest Girl in Town" (Cole Porter) sung by Marlene Dietrich in *Stage Fright*.

"Third Man Theme" (Anton Karas) from *Third Man*.

"A Kiss to Build a Dream On" (Bert Kalmar, Harry Ruby, Oscar Hammerstein II) from *The Strip*.

"I'm Late" (Bob Hilliard, Sammy Fain) from *Alice in Wonderland*.

"Because You're Mine" (Cahn, Brodszky) sung by Mario Lanza in *Because You're Mine*.

"Make 'Em Laugh" (Arthur Freed, Nacio Herb Brown) performed by Gene Kelly, Donald O'Connor in *Singin' in the Rain*.

"High Noon" (Ned Washington, Dimitri Tiomkin) from *High Noon*.

"Lavender Blue" (Elliot Daniel, Larry Morey) from *So Dear to My Heart*.

"No Two People," "Thumbelina," "Inchworm," "Wonderful Copenhagen," "Anywhere I Wander," "Ugly Duckling" (Frank Loesser) sung by Danny Kaye in *Hans Christian Andersen*.

"Blue Pacific Blues" (Lester Lee, Ned Washington) from *Miss Sadie Thompson*.

"Secret Love" (Sammy Fain, Paul Francis Webster) sung by Doris Day in *Calamity Jane*.

"The High and the Mighty" (Dimitri Tiomkin, Ned Washington) from *The High and the Mighty*.

"Hold My Hand" (Jack Lawrence, Richard Myers) from *Susan Slept Here*.

"The Man That Got Away," "Gotta Have Me Go With You," "Here's What I'm Here For," "Lose That Long Face" (Harold Arlen, Ira Gershwin) sung by Judy Garland in *A Star is Born*.

"Love Is a Many Splendored Thing" (Fain, Webster) from *Love Is a Many Splendored Thing*.

"The Tender Trap" (Sammy Cahn, Jimmy Van Heusen) sung by Frank Sinatra in *The Tender Trap*.

"Unchained Melody" (Alex North, Hy Zaret) from *Unchained*.

"Thee I Love" (Tiomkin, Webster) from *Friendly Persuasion*.

"Que Sera Sera" (Jay Livingston, Ray Evans) sung by Doris Day in *The Man Who Knew Too Much*.

"All the Way" (Cahn, Van Heusen) sung by Frank Sinatra in *The Joker Is Wild*.

"April Love" (Fain, Webster) sung by Pat Boone in *April Love*.

"Tammy" (Ray Evans, Jay Livingston) from *Tammy and the Bachelor*.

"Wild Is the Wind" (Tiomkin, Washington) from *Wild Is the Wind*.

"Pete Kelly's Blues" (Sammy Cahn, Ray Heindorf) sung by Ella Fitzgerald in *Pete Kelly's Blues*.

"Siamese Cat Song" (Peggy Lee, Sonny Burke) from *Lady and the Tramp*.

"Baby, You Knock Me Out," "I Like Myself," "Time for Parting" (Betty Comden, Adolph Green, André Previn) performed by Gene Kelly, Dan Dailey, Michael Kidd in *It's Always Fair Weather*.

"Indiscretion" (Sammy Cahn, Paul Weston, Alessandro Cicognini) from *Indiscretions of an American Wife*.

"Love Makes the World Go Round" (Dorcas Cochran, Oscar Straus) from *La Ronde*.

"Love Theme from *La Strada*" (Don Raye, N. Rota) from *La Strada*.

"Smile" (John Turner, Geoffrey Parsons, Charlie Chaplin) from *Modern Times*.

"Sobbin' Women," "Wonderful, Wonderful Day," "When You're in Love," "Spring, Spring, Spring" (Johnny Mercer, Gene dePaul) performed by Howard Keel, Jane Powell, others, in *Seven Brides for Seven Brothers*.

"An Occasional Man" (Hugh Martin, Ralph Blane) from *The Girl Rush*.

"Theme from *Picnic*" (George Duning); NOTE: Steve Allen later wrote lyrics, and the theme was usually coupled with the old popular song, "Moonglow," as it had been in the film *Picnic*.

"A Woman in Love" (Frank Loesser) from *Guys and Dolls*.

"Anastasia" (Paul Francis Webster, Alfred Newman) from *Anastasia*.

"Around the World" (Harold Adamson, Victor Young) from *Around the World in 80 Days*.

"Love Me Tender" (Elvis Presley, Vera Matson) from *Love Me Tender*. (Since this song is actually an adaptation of the old Civil War ballad, "Aura Lea," it probably shouldn't be included here. But let's give Elvis one number in this list.)

"You're Sensational," "Who Wants To Be a Millionaire?" (Cole Porter) both sung by Frank Sinatra, the latter with Celeste Holm, in *High Society*.

"Fascination" (Dick Manning, F. D. Marchetti),

also an adaptation of a very old song but passing as a new number for *Love in the Afternoon.*

"Song from *Moulin Rouge*" (William Engvick, Georges Auric) from *Moulin Rouge.*

"Cherry Pink and Apple Blossom White" (Mack David, Louiguy) from *Underwater.*

"My Resistance Is Low" (Adamson, Carmichael) from *The Las Vegas Story.*

"Hi-Lili, Hi-Lo" (Helen Deutsch, Bronislow Kaper) from *Lili.*

"When I Fall in Love" (Edward Heyman, Victor Young) from *One Minute to Zero.*

"Anna" (William Engvick, R. Vatro) from *Anna.*

"Eternally" ("The Terry Theme") (Geoffrey Parsons, Charles Chaplin) from *Limelight.*

"Face to Face" (Cahn, Fain) performed by Jane Powell, Gordon MacRae in *Three Sailors and a Girl.*

"Ruby" (Mitchell Parish, Heinz Roemheld) from *Ruby Gentry.*

"The Long, Hot Summer" (Sammy Cahn, Alex North) from *The Long, Hot Summer.*

"Thank Heaven for Little Girls," "Gigi," "The Night They Invented Champagne," "I Remember It Well" (Alan Jay Lerner, Frederick Loewe), sung by Leslie Caron, Louis Jourdan, Maurice Chevalier, Hermione Gingold in *Gigi.*

"Almost in Your Arms" (Jay Livingston, Ray Evans) from *Houseboat.*

"A Certain Smile" (Fain, Webster) from *A Certain Smile.*

"A Summer Place" (Max Steiner) from *A Summer Place.*

"Faraway Part of Town" (André Previn, Dory Langdon) from *Pepe.*

"Green Leaves of Summer" (Tiomkin, Webster) from *The Alamo.*

"Never on Sunday" (Manos Hadjidakis) from *Never on Sunday.*

"The Facts of Life" (Johnny Mercer) from *The Facts of Life.*

"Moon River" (Mercer, Henry Mancini, from *Breakfast at Tiffany's.*

"Tender Is the Night" (Fain, Webster) from *Tender Is the Night.*

"Walk on the Wild Side" (Elmer Bernstein, Mack David) from *Walk on the Wild Side.*

"Days of Wine and Roses" (Mancini, Mercer) from *Days of Wine and Roses.*

"The Longest Day" (Paul Anka) from *The Longest Day.*

"Call Me Irresponsible" (Van Heusen, Cahn) from *Papa's Delicate Condition.*

"Charade" (Mancini, Mercer) from *Charade.*

"More" (Riz Ortolani, N. Newell) from *Mondo Cane.*

"So Little Time" (Tiomkin, Webster) from *55 Days at Peking.*

"Sunday in New York" (Peter Nero, Carroll Coates) from *Sunday in New York.*

"From Russia With Love" (Lionel Bart, John Barry) from *From Russia With Love.*

"Chim-Chim-Cheree," "Supercalifragilisticarpialidocious" (Richard M. Sherman, Robert B. Sherman) sung by Julie Andrews in *Mary Poppins.*

"Emily" (Johnny Mercer, Johnny Mandel) from *Americanization of Emily.*

"Dear Heart" (Mancini, Evans, Livingston) from *Dear Heart.*

"Wives and Lovers" (David, Bacharach) from *Wives and Lovers.*

"Can't Buy Me Love," "And I Love Her," "Tell Me Why," "This Boy" (John Lennon, Paul McCartney) as performed by The Beatles in *A Hard Day's Night.*

"Pink Panther Theme" (Mercer, Mancini) from *The Pink Panther.*

"Goldfinger" (John Barry, Anthony Newley, Leslie Bricusse) sung by Shirley Bassey in *Goldfinger.*

"Pass Me By" (Cy Coleman, Carolyn Leigh) from *Father Goose.*

"Goodbye Charlie" (Dory Langdon, André Previn) from *Goodbye Charlie.*

"Where Love Has Gone" (Cahn, Van Heusen) from *Where Love Has Gone.*

"My Kind of Town" (Cahn, Van Heusen) sung by Frank Sinatra in *Robin and the Seven Hoods.*

"Topkapi" (Manos Hadjidakis) from *Topkapi.*

"I Will Wait for You" (Jacques Demy, Michel Legrand) from *The Umbrellas of Cherbourg.*

"Shadow of Your Smile" (Johnny Mandel, Paul Francis Webster) from *The Sandpiper.*

"Help," "A Ticket to Ride" (Lennon, McCartney) sung by The Beatles in *Help!.*

"What's New, Pussycat?" (Hal David, Burt Bacharach) from *What's New, Pussycat?.*

"Promise Her Anything" (Hal David, Burt Bacharach) from *Promise Her Anything.*

"The Sweetheart Tree" (Mercer, Mancini) from *The Great Race.*

"Sinner Man" (Billy Barberis, Bobby Weinstein, B. Hart, Teddy Randazzo) from *Marriage on the Rocks.*

"Strangers in the Night" (Bert Kaempfert, Ed Snyder, Chuck Singleton) from *A Man Could Get Killed.*

"You're Going to Hear From Me" (by André and Dory Previn) from *Inside Daisy Clover.*

"Alfie" (by Burt Bacharach, Hal David) from *Alfie.*

Index

256